Bouncepreneurs

Successfully Bounce Back After Business Failure

By Michael Allen

Dedicated to Wioletta my smiling friend and biggest loss

1 Welcome to the Beginning of Your Bounce Back

1.1. Introduction

Welcome to the Bouncepreneur Movement.

This book aims to help you feel much better after losing an earlier business. It then goes on to help you back to success and happiness.

A simple plan. I hope you can agree.

Most people reading this book have been bought it by a friend or loved one. You are likely to be low, broke and in denial. Do read on.

Bouncepreneurs has a solid plan and place for you. Join us.

Now then, I will not tell you a long (and frankly boring) story about myself. So you can relax. I will just let you read my book and form your own opinion of my personal story.

So….

Your business has failed

Your latest new product or service has bombed

You are fearful about your future

Then you have come to the right place. Become one of us. You are amongst friends.

Welcome to Bouncepreneurs.

1.2. Leper Mentality

Failed entrepreneurs are lepers!

Society loves start-ups, loves innovation. Politicians want photos and champagne. They openly lie about failure rates of businesses.

More businesses fail than succeed. Behind every failure is a family, individual or group.

Our global economy pushes more and more people towards self-employment and small business ventures. Innovators are told not to fear failure. Government pushes everyone to start up, women, ethnic minorities, the poor, the Third World, ex-Military, ex-Convicts –even kids!

So does big business. Failure is also a big business. Ask an entrepreneur how much the interest rate is on their car or credit card before and after failure!

It is a huge money machine. You know that already!

But most businesses do fail! They Do! Leaving many in a bad place financially and mentally.

With the universal rise of credit rating a failed business can become a failed life!

So a business failure can make us feel like Lepers.

And maybe there are more Lepers than non-Lepers.

And we have to pay far more for credit, struggle to get work and generally get treated like second class citizens.

I see this clearly and say NO MORE!

So in this book I have set out to the best of my ability a personal recovery plan for "Failed" Entrepreneurs.

But not to get out of this Leper community back into the establishments "Good Boys and Girls Club." No!

I hope to see a tribe of people and supporters who REALLY understand part of being an entrepreneur can be failure. Not just to pay lip service to it! I hope to see people who behave ethically and work together to aid recovery, learn from the experience and most importantly of all.

DO NOT ALLOW THEMSELVES TO FEEL ASHAMED OR DISGRACED

Finally my own Entrepreneurial Recovery was fuelled by anger. Yes anger. After years of success, employing people and export success I became a "Failed Entrepreneur."

I was in the Leper Colony.

After too many dark days I decided to fight back. I do not care if I rough up the "peace and harmony" views of Big Business, the farce that is Corporate Social Responsibility, Economic Development Agencies and Government who ignore the Elephant in the Room.

I want to help "Failed Entrepreneurs" back to Wealth and Happiness. For this to happen the Lepers have to rebel.

Become a Bouncepreneur – Bounce Back to Wealth and Happiness.

1.3. Overcoming Venture Failure

Part One of this book helps you to deal with your immediate situation after the failure of your venture, or previous business.

My MAIN goal here is to ensure that you emerge from the pain and grief of this situation as quickly as possible. I seek to guide you to selecting the right path for your future,

By providing a thorough explanation and understanding of what others in your position have experienced, I hope to get you moving forward into happiness and prosperity as soon as possible.

So in Part One of this book I cover the following:-

<u>Realisation and Realities</u> – to help you see your position more clearly and that all is not lost.

<u>Understanding Entrepreneurial Grief</u> – I show you how Entrepreneurial Grief is as real as losing a family member and how it can really mess you up for years. But it does not have to!

<u>How to Recover from Entrepreneurial Grief</u> – well I am not going to leave you stranded am I? You can recover and prosper faster with my method. It is practical, real and no nonsense.

<u>Choosing the Right Recovery Path for You</u> – Bouncepreneurs assists Entrepreneurs Bounce Back to success and prosperity. But I understand this may not be the right path right now for everyone. Your options are explored.

1.4. Bounce Back – Becoming a Black Belt Bouncepreneur

In the second part of the book, which although serious has a few smiles for you too. I show you how to Bounce Back to prosperity and happiness.

You will be introduced to a series of 7 Kangaroo Guides to help you prepare, launch and succeed with your Bounce Back business. Each has their own personality and lessons to share with you.

Kangaroos are commonly associated with boxing. But as a confidant to all Kangaroos myself and being able to converse with them telepathically, I can actually tell you that Karate is actually their first love. (I hope that is your first smile!)

Each of your Kangaroo Guides wears a Karate belt from white to black. As you read their Guidance you will be given a series of exercises to complete. As you complete these tasks you will climb up through the belts. Your ultimate goal is the Black Belt.

A Black Belt Bouncepreneur is a fully recovered entrepreneur who has successfully launched a new venture within 6 months. Yes 6 months!

The belts are there to rebuild your confidence, show you just how far you have progressed and of course empower you to discuss your challenges with other Bouncepreneurs in a commonly understood framework.

Imagine the Kangaroo Guides as a series of friends. I warn you some a warmer than others. But they are all you friends. But remember Kangaroos are tough animals. They have to be, they face attack by dingoes and lots of fences aimed at restricting their movement.

I guess this is why the Maker designed Kangaroos only to go forward. Yes that is right Kangaroos cannot go backwards. They really cannot. Only forward. Just like you from now on.

One other thing about Kangaroos, they start by taking little hops, slow and cautious, but when they turn on the afterburners, they can move AND they can move fast far further than other speedsters of the natural world. You will be the same after reading this book. You will know when to be cautious and take small experimental hops.

I promise when you see your clear path you are going to go for it AT PACE! Plus you are going to be able to do this for a sustained period. When you do stop, your plan will allow you to rest and not keep needing to race about.

So the Kangaroo Guides you will meet are

White – to help you blanch your mind of past failures

Yellow – will help you develop bright new ideas

Orange – ensures you go with the right idea with the 7 Orange Fences Test

Blue – brings you discipline and professionalism

Green – helps you too launch a new business effectively at very low cost

Brown –Capability Brown guides you to being very capable in key business areas

Black – You have made it. Time to consolidate and become a serial Bouncepreneur

1.5. Key Concepts Explained

Bouncepreneur –a Bouncepreneur is an entrepreneur whose previous venture has failed, but he or she is working towards rebuilding their wealth and happiness through the Bounce Back process.

Bounce Back – the recovery of an entrepreneur whose previous venture has failed back to happiness and prosperity. This involves recovering from Entrepreneurial Grief, launching a business, replacing yourself in all key roles, becoming a non-executive Chairperson and finally becoming a serial entrepreneur.

SUDGO – Scale Up/Duplicate/Get Out of Operations this is the core decision making concept behind choosing an effective business venture to pursue. The SUDGO model is based on a 6 month period! Yes 6 months!

HugeCorp – is Bouncepreneurs collective description for global and large enterprises, the establishment and government support agencies ignoring failed entrepreneurs. It is not complimentary. Bouncepreneurs are simply a completely separate tribe. With vastly different approaches to life, success and community spirit.

Dingoes – Dingoes kill Kangaroos. They hunt in packs. They are the Kangaroo Guides and Bouncepreneurs mortal enemy. Dingoes are cunning, smile before they bite and are to be avoided at all costs. They offer entrepreneurs and not just Bouncepreneurs services and advice which benefit the Dingoes and the Dingoes alone.

Bouncepreneur Movement – all Bouncepreneurs and enlightened governments, government agencies and enterprises who seek a fairer approach to innovators and entrepreneurs who fail.

Bouncepreneur Tribe – the Tribe all Bouncepreneurs belong to. Successful Bouncepreneurs feel responsible for helping those in Entrepreneurial Grief recover. The tribe cherishes personal pride in achieving a Bounce Back. We recognise the success in others achieving Bounce Back. We give open and honest public testimony of the realities of Entrepreneurial Failure and Bounce Back. Finally we display the Black Kangaroo device whenever possible to promote understanding of our movement.

Timeline – A Bouncepreneur recovery experience has five main phases

   i. Failure of your previous venture – Red Kangaroo phase – you are totally alone.
  ii. Entrepreneurial Grief – broke, depression, disbelief, kidding yourself – generally a very bad time which can last years.
 iii. Grief Recovery – the period when you overcome Entrepreneurial Grief and start to think about Bouncing Back to wealth and happiness
  iv. 7 Kangaroo Guides – you meet, learn from and receive a series of recognition belts from white to black from your mentors and friends - the Bouncepreneur Kangaroo Guides.
   v. Black Belt Bouncepreneur – this is the ultimate achievement for a Bouncepreneur. You have established a successful business, you are not involved in the operations of that business. You have a salary and are building net personal worth to invest in other ventures. You are becoming a serial entrepreneur.

OK let's bounce on….

2 Realisation and Realities

2.1 Objective of this Chapter

I aim to have an immediate impact on the way you view and face the Realities of your personal situation.

The failure of your last venture does not make YOU a failure.

GOT THAT?

They are not the same thing AT ALL!

My goal is to do this with the heart of a trusted friend and the vision of a talent scout who can still see your enormous potential as an entrepreneur.

The quicker and more decisively we help you reach this cool, cold understanding - the better and the faster your Entrepreneur Recovery.

Right now you may be in the Red Phase – your business has failed or is about to fail.

The one reaction I don't want to this Chapter is "I don't need to be told that!" or "Don't you think I already get that!" Although I do understand why you might think that.

Do yourself a great favour. Sit down, take a few deep breaths. Suspend cynicism, frustration and concentrate on what I have to say for 20 minutes.

Thank you. Let's go forward

The objective of this Chapter is to help Entrepreneurs whose venture failed move forward, by helping you to gain total clarity about your own situation now!

<u>Not the clarity you may think you have</u>, but a sharper clarity based on the experience of entrepreneurs who have walked this path before you.

- Realise you are in a Grieving Process like you have lost an immediate member of your family.
- To encourage you to accept the realities of now.
- To plant some ideas about an Entrepreneurial Bounce Back

At the end of this Chapter you should have a sharper Realisation that your position is far from unique. BUT you are carrying significant grief, <u>as well</u> as real-life day to day problems I know are pretty grim, forward.

If you have bought this book, my guess is you are looking to be helped. But I know through my own experience that you may be very agitated at the moment. You will be wracked with worry over your finances, your future, and your family if you have one or keeping your girlfriend/boyfriend in your new situation.

As entrepreneurs whose venture has failed you will be in a state of transition. By transition I mean getting your mind around the fact that your old business is gone. Finished! Flat! Finito! Fin!

You may be thinking that "I fully accept that and I have moved on." But the reality is often different.

Try to see your situation in a holistic fashion from 360 degrees. By seeing it this way you can better make an Accelerated Recovery or Bounce Back.

What I have found ALWAYS to be the case with recently failed entrepreneurs is that they are often in one or more of the following states:-

- Believing the old business is still going to be ok (even though the receivers have taken the equipment or shut you out of your building!)
- Desperately trying to create a life-boat company (a copy of the failed business in all but name).
- Effectively a break-down, very depressed, feeling lost and not looking after physical health very well. Maybe even drinking or worse.
- Frantically selling possessions to keep up appearances of success. Often selling valuable items for a fraction of their worth.

2.2. The Idea of Entrepreneurial Grief

Entrepreneurial Grief is a major part of this book. For good reason. We cover it in much more detail in the next chapter.

This Grief is very real and tangible, if you have lost a venture you will be feeling it.

It has been likened to losing an immediate member of your family.

It is a big deal. But the news is good. YOU CAN LEARN SO MUCH FROM IT

At the same time you are suffering this Grief, you have a number of serious financial, direction and possibly relationship issues to contend with. So life will be challenging.

So why do I focus on it so much. Understanding it, picking out the valuable lessons from the mirages and leaving the rubbish and garbage behind is essential.

ESSENTIAL.

I would suggest you start to think about this Entrepreneurial Grief like malaria. I want to give you inoculations now to keep it away for life. Otherwise, it will just keep coming back, time after time.

Like malaria, when you recover you can think the feeling of losing your business is behind you, then bang you are flat out in bed again. Speaking with real Bouncepreneurs the average duration of transition is 12-24 months. It can be much longer and in some cases a transition is never fully made.

I believe my own recovery has taken 4 years.

So like malaria, you are never fully cured of the illness. But you can turn the learning and experience to your advantage and later when you have made a full recovery you can help others.

2.3. The Typical Pressures You Will Be Feeling Right Now

I understand you are facing terrible pressures right now. Some of them might be:-

Letting Go - you have to let the old venture and mistakes go. Only then can you start to focus on moving forward.

Playing Things Over and Over in Your Mind - you need to openly confront the mistakes you made and give yourself the chance to feel it all. Otherwise, anxiety will start to linger in the back of your mind and the soft hiss of failure will continue.

Money – essentially you are very short of it. Your personal finances are very tight and likely you used your savings while you tried to keep your business afloat. In short a deeply unpleasant time.

Debt – the business still owes money. Even though you have liquidated some of your suppliers and customers are very angry with you and won't go away.

Relationships – If you have a girlfriend or boyfriend and it is quite a new relationship, you may have shielded your financial situation. But now the time has come to be more open and admit that your business has failed. You may not be sure what impact your poverty will have on your relationship.

Family – You know your long term partner or spouse is worried about the future. Perhaps they work with you in the business. Your children have been having fewer and fewer treats and birthday presents were minimal. Your parents are worried

Friends – Some keep asking why you are not coming out so much over the weekend. Others tease you about being a hermit. The good ones have asked how you are doing and been confidants

Business administration – Even though your business has closed, there still seems to be a lot of administration to do. The tax people want information, Companies House, your former landlord.

Food on table – Simply filling the fridge is becoming a challenge. You've started selling possessions on eBay to make ends meet.

Home – You have not paid your mortgage for a year and repossession is looming

Car – You had a lovely Mercedes on contract hire. But the recovery guys took it away last week. The neighbours keep asking where your lovely car has gone.

Social pressure spending – That family wedding is coming up. Everyone is going to Portugal for the celebration. You don't have the money and the heart to tell them you cannot go.

2.4. Important Issues

I will take you through some important issues. These are

a. The Last Gasps from Your Failed Business
b. Some Destructive Ideas You Must Clear Out of Your Head
c. Communicating with Partners
d. Not Being Seen as a Broken Man or Woman
e. Some Things to Start Thinking About in Terms of Recovery

2.5. The Last Gasps from Your Failed Business

Lifeboat Companies

The use of life boat companies is of course widespread. They are attractive for two main reasons, one good and one deeply flawed in my view.

Firstly if the business has a core of profitability that has been dragged down by other unprofitable products or services, then the good bit may be worth saving and using as a Bounce Back business. But it really has to offer the potential of being a WEALTH ENGINE.

Think about the SUDGO

Ask yourself this:-

SU Can you scale up?

D Can you duplicate it?

GO Can you Get Out/Is it Getoutable Can it run without me?

If the answer to ANY of these questions is NO then let it sink. To do otherwise is to put yourself back into a situation where you simply will not be able to make it grow and yourself financially independent and rich. We talk much more about this later in the book. You may wish to run your life boat business idea past the Yellow and Orange Kangaroo Guides before trying to go forward with a previously failed business again.

If it meets all three Wealth Engine criteria and you are not deliberately avoid paying creditors to go forward with this vehicle then it may be a viable route.

The **second reason** that people go forward with a Lifeboat company is not sound. It is simply being dictated by your past lifestyle and familiarity. Many are institutionalised to living within their own company. Many truck owner-drivers are in this mode. Preferring to earn very, very poor salaries and stay behind the wheel and in a lifestyle they know.

Too often the new Lifeboat business' simply represents a minor name change and of course the shedding of debt. I have seen Lifeboat business start again with the same toxic staff, same flawed locations and same poor liquidity. I myself have used a Lifeboat business and even though it was an agonising process, I simply did not improve or overhaul the business model. So it failed again.

So if you are thinking of moving forward with a Lifeboat business you must be able to answer these questions to 100 percent certainty.

a. To what extent is my vanity and pride keeping me in this business?
b. What is fundamentally different about the profitability of this business compared to the original one?
c. What is my plan to transform it?
d. What fall out should I expect from customers after they become aware the original business has failed?
e. Will my suppliers continue to trade with me going forward/are there alternative suppliers?
f. Am I treating my creditors fairly by moving forward in this way?

Still Trading

Failed Entrepreneurs, often continue to trade in their failed project. Maybe you are? Most often it is desperation, or denial of the facts.

But if you are still trading in a limited company after liquidation you are behaving improperly. The business entity, raw materials, goods and everything else in that business simply are not yours to trade. It is that simple. In the UK, my country, for example, it is called trading whilst insolvent, insolvent trading or wrongful trading. It will have similarities in your own country. Strictly speaking here in the UK, wrongful trading only applies to company Directors, whereas Insolvent Trading can be undertaken by individuals such as sole traders.

The main message is there is a criminal facet to this which should be avoided at all costs.

But this is not rocket science is it? If you carry on running your business, whether it is incorporated or not, most likely you are breaking a law. So don't do it.

There are other circumstances of course such as someone who owes nobody money, but cannot sell their materials or stock at the prices they need to break even. In this scenario the business owner already owns the stock and may decide to offload it at a loss to provide some badly needed income.

But the risks you are taking include:-

- Being disqualified as an officer of the company (or a future company). This could really bite you in years to come.
- Being made personally liable for the debts of the business.

What is the risk? Well if you are accused by a liquidator of a company of Wrongful Trading then as Director you could be personally liable for the damage the company suffered during a period of Wrongful Trading - so do not do it!!

But most importantly of all, every day you spend continuing to trade in an already failed project is a day further from making a proper Entrepreneurial Recovery and achieving Wealth and Happiness.

Waiting for that Business Saving Deal

In some businesses a single deal can be transformational. This is especially true in consultancy businesses. Sometimes one can wait, wait and wait some more for a deal that simply does not come.

There may well be a buyer within a major company or government organisation saying "it just has one more person to sign it off and we will get the PO across to you." Truth is they never come in, do they?

But there are many individuals after the business has failed, still waiting for this one project. Especially in consulting and private services.

Well I say this to you. As a private consultant unless you are a miracle worker the only lifestyle you will have until the day you retire (in poverty) will be one of anxiety.

Waiting for that one big deal has already cost you one business. Let that thinking go and set out a new business model that is Scalable, Repeatable and Able to run without you.

2.6. Some Destructive Ideas You Must Clear Out of Your Head

Spending like you still have business money

You may still have monthly payments going out for services you were using in your business. As a small business owner you may not be too aware of them. Well get aware! They will suck your capital out from under you. Some examples are:-

- Trade association memberships
- Monthly payments for hosting and email accounts for your old business
- LinkedIn memberships
- Rolling AdWords advertising
- Building insurance
- Employers liability insurances
- Retained lawyers and retained accountants

These all need to be closed down quickly and decisively. A close inspection of your business and personal bank statement for the last year will identify any loose spending items.

Stop those direct debits, cancel those subscriptions and make sure those social media advertising sites haven't committed you to unexpected spending in the future.

The Scale of Money Business v Personal

Business owners often lose perspective between the cost of personal purchases and business purchases. Generally a purchase through a business is not scrutinised as carefully as a personal purchase, especially when the owner is really busy.

Think about when you bought the office fridge or even kettle versus the one in your kitchen.

I will give you a further example. The cost of a monthly subscription to LinkedIn is equivalent to the weekly grocery shop for a single business person. What is more important to you now you are without a business and without an income?

Now you are in transition it is vitally important you cull all costs associated to your old business.

There is only one scale of money for you now, your personal Net Worth.

Get out of all costs associated with you old business and do it fast!

<u>Telling People White Lies</u>

Because of the culture of shame, no-one wants to tell their social circle their business has changed.

But you have no need to justify or explain yourself to anyone. To anyone.

Some examples of when you might tell a fib to avoid "the shame."

- When you sell your car (or the finance company takes it back!) and you are running an old banger of a car, it is embarrassing. You can be sure neighbours will ask, what happened to the Mercedes?
- Or you have not been seen in the local bar or restaurant for many weeks.
- Or people have seen your shop, house or office with a To Let or For Sale Sign Outside.
- Or you cannot take that new girlfriend or boyfriend out to the New Year's Eve Party
- Or your children ask why they cannot go to Spain this summer

Don't tell people lies. Tell the truth. Or tell them to mind their own business.

With Family - I talk about communicating with your family shortly. But the advice here is hold a family meeting. Be open and be a leader.

With Friends – again be open. Tell them, you may need to keep a lower profile socially for a while as money is going to be tight. Your real friends will rally to you. Expect a few surprises here. I certainly did. People I least expected came through for me in many unexpected ways. A few disappointed me. But they were a minority. People are good. If they weren't the world would not function.

With Children- Children value one thing more than money and gifts. It is time with their mother or father having fun. Seize this opportunity, even stroppy teenagers will support you if you are straight with them. Find something your child really likes doing and do it with them – it might be as simple as drawing Manga comics or learning the guitar.

With Boyfriends or Girlfriends – be open. Give this person the facts about your situation. Don't stay away from them if you cannot afford to take them out. If they love you, they will make allowances. They will help you. But it is important you show respect. Be honest. Don't so or say silly things like "you would be better off without me" or be a victim. No one likes to be in a relationship with someone who looks broken. Don't allow yourself to be seen as a "Broken Man" or "Broken Woman".

I am no relationship coach, but my advice is be honest and show you love this person and that you are moving forward. If this person does not want you despite your honesty and integrity, then you are better off without them. If you do get dumped over a business failure (it happens believe me), I strongly recommend watching Indian Actor Varun Pruthi's great story on YouTube – and it is a true story. As Varun says "Use Your Pain, Don't Let Your Pain Use You."

Finally, when it comes to telling lies to cover up your shame. Just don't do it:-

A good phrase to use to people is this (always with a smile!)

"As an Entrepreneur I understand I may have ups and downs as I move forward to success. These are of course my own concern and no-one else's. I am sure you understand that don't you?"

Within your family and circle of loved ones you can say:-

"Look, if we want to be prosperous we have to learn. I have learnt some big lessons recently. Things will be a little tough for a while, but not for too long. The important thing is we love each other, stay honest and work together to move forward."

<u>Job won't be hard to get</u>

One of the biggest shocks I had myself was how challenging it was to get a job to pay those bills.

You may be surprised to read that I do not recommend that everyone goes back to business ownership in the short term. A temporary or permanent job in some cases is the best route.

But it may not be as easy as expected to get a job! As someone who had significant business experience, reasonably up to date digital skills and quite good qualifications I was in for a wakeup call. It was not that easy. Also my attitude did not help. I kept thinking "what the hell am I doing here in interviews at banks and big companies." So, unfortunately getting a job at the level you might expect may be a lot harder than you think.

The biggest issue you will face in applying to major businesses in the Applicant Screening Software linked to Credit Scoring. More of this below. But first to share my own experience in job hunting

- I had a good degree but no MBA. You need MBA's nowadays
- Business almost universally wanted specific qualifications in marketing and project management that I did not have
- My age 50+, I saw that many organisations believed I would not be digitally savvy. I was, but it did not seem to matter.
- I did not do well in psychometric testing. I still don't think the results reflected my personality well, but I was not the recruiter.
- As a long term self-employed person I had to be both candidate and referee for myself. Recruiters did not seem to like this very much.
- I was in not near a major city and jobs nearby were limited. A move was required.
- The salaries I needed required specific in company (large company) experience, I did not have it, but others did.

If you have weak credit rating (which after a business failure is likely) you need to be aware of a major waste of your time in seeking employment.

But perhaps one of the greatest barriers to you finding a job is the Applicant Tracking Systems Linked to Credit Rating. Sometimes these are called Applicant Tracking Systems, Human Resources Information Software or Recruitment Software, different names for systems that support job applications. Application tracking systems ALSO provide the opportunity for corporate recruiters to link or handshake with credit referencing agencies. The terms and conditions on recruiter's websites do state that credit rating may be used. But it is in small print and clearly NOT transparent enough.

You may write one bespoke application or CV after another to major (safe job) enterprises to secure your future.

This may well be a **total** and **complete** waste of time.

A TOTAL waste of time.

Now I am not suggesting that credit rating should not be used when recruiting for roles involving financial management. Of course not!

But, it is not reasonable to allow many individuals to be spending hours writing bespoke CV's and applications for specific roles that they are automatically going to be excluded from on credit rating.

Is it a post credit crunch inequality? Should it be compared to racial or sex discrimination?

If you have recently lost your business and are unemployed, you may be claiming social security or unemployment benefit. You need to find work.

Isn't it reasonable that you have an opportunity to rebuild your life, work hard for an employer and gain a decent salary?

To be judged on skills and experience is fair. To be excluded from roles WITHOUT key financial responsibilities such as a Financial Director, is simply not fair.

I have three recommendations for organisations using credit rating in candidate screening

- Consider if credit rating is appropriate for all your job postings
- Clarify your position on credit rating. Don't let people apply for roles that require strong credit ratings. They need a job, so don't let them waste time.
- Advertise jobs as friendly towards people rebuilding their finances

2.7. Not Communicating Situation with Family, Partner or Loved Ones

Keep Your Partner Informed

It surprises me how many entrepreneurs who have lost a business do not communicate the fact for several months after the event. Even hiding the fact that the business has failed from their immediate family (just like Gerald in the movie The Full Monty who hasn't told his wife he has been unemployed for six months. He is frantic with worry and she is planning their skiing holiday).

Don't Bottle it All Up

Business failure will drain you in a big way. But failure is all part of innovation and learning, so do not be too hard on yourself. What is really the important thing at this stage is to release those negative and destructive feelings you have inside your system. By getting rid or reducing them you can stabilise and face key decisions for your life and happiness. But you must not keep your feelings trapped without release or you WILL explode.

It will be your loved ones who get it!

Just a small trigger will lead to a huge outburst of anger. Then having yelled at your spouse, parent or child you will feel tremendous guilt and you will feel even more lost.

Explain what is happening

You have to explain the realities of the situation to your partner as early and openly as possible. There is no point in hiding the facts. You are not being heroic. If your relationship is dependent on your financial success than ask yourself this question.

Is it time to move on from this relationship too?

But most often people who love you will stick by you. They will encourage, chastise, push and pull you back to success.

All you have to do in return is show that you appreciate the support and take a leadership role. Show you have a plan. Don't look like a Broken Man or Broken Woman.

But if you hide the truth I promise you one thing. It will be the end of your relationship. Your heroic lies will HAVE to get bigger and bigger and you will get found out.

Then you may end up losing your loved ones as well as your business.

Do not risk it. Be honest and be straight.

But one of the great things about couples running businesses and contrary to what you might expect is that they often really pull together once a business has failed. Often one goes into a full time job, freeing the partner to launch a new business. Then once successful the one in employment most often returns to assist.

We talk more about how to handle your Bounce Back with partners, family and children a little later.

2.8. Broken Man or Broken Woman

Are you familiar with personal branding? Well if you are walking around looking stressed, acting stressed and generally behaving in a stressed way then you have the personal brand of a Broken Man or Broken Woman.

How does that look to your loved ones?

It makes them worry about you, the situation and your relationship. It is that simple.

Mix into that a few too many beers or a bottle of Chardonnay every night and not only will you start to look heavy, your wits will slow too.

So my advice to you is to think about your own personal brand.

Do not look like a Broken Man or Broken Woman.

The failure of your last venture does not make YOU a failure. GOT THAT? They are not the same thing AT ALL!

You want to get past this business failure and back to success right?

In fact you may not have been THAT successful at ANY point with your last business model. It may have been nothing more than just an adequate job!

So now you are planning not just to Bounce Back but to go on to real wealth and success

So let's think about your Personal Brand.

Your Personal Brand Might Be Some of These Things

Calm – even though others might lose their heads in this situation. You are not going to, are you? You are the personification of calm even under this pressure.

In Control – you have a plan. You are going to use the Bouncepreneurs Recovery Plan. You are going to get a Bouncepreneur Black Belt as worn by Kangaroos! (More of that later). So you most definitely have control of you own destiny.

Smart – You are going to dress to impress every day, even if you live alone and are single. Wear clean, professional clothes. Dress for work.

Fit – You are under pressure. There is no doubt of that. So you must be fit. The only way you are going to get that stress out of your body is exercise. Maybe some meditation too. Use your Entrepreneur Recovery time to get fit. Personally I used swimming. Each person to their own preference. But I would recommend swimming for several reasons. Firstly it makes you very fit. Secondly a gentle swim gives you time to meditate and flush out negative feelings. Thirdly if you get involved with a swim, you will meet new people, often triathletes who you will find generally more positive than the guys down the pub.

It never ceases to amaze me how different people treat you when you are clearly in good physical condition. It takes time, but get that stress out and make fitness part of your daily plan.

Be Yourself – In the famous British Sci-Fi Comedy Red Dwarf the crew rebuild a damaged robot called Kryten. The only thing they are not able to restore is his personality. Thereafter Kryten is extremely boring. Don't let business failure crush your personality. Be true to yourself and let this experience enrichen you as a person, not humble you.

Realistic – Obviously throughout this whole process you must be realistic. You cannot afford to be anything else. The reality is that financial pressure will be all around you. Stay organised with your mail, your filing and your correspondence.

Just because you cannot pay your bills right now, is no excuse for not knowing what they are.

Laser-Like – Last but not least, you need to start behaving in a laser-like fashion. Cut out those activities, people and vices that do not serve your recovery well. Focus as much as possible on an organised work day, keeping your creditors informed and under control (even if not being paid) and maintaining you mental and physical wellbeing.

2.9. Summary

In Summary of this chapter on Realisation and Realities, let's look at the Five F's. I also want to give you some small thoughts about a Bounce Back. But not full throttle just yet.

Future

- You will have a brighter, happier, richer future than where you are right now
- You can be future focused
- Your past is gone. No matter you once had a Bentley, forget it you are where you stand now.
- You owe it to your loved ones to give them a future and to move forward in an accelerated fashion
- Don't start your future in 5 years, or 3 years or next year. Start now!

Family, Friends and Faith

- Your family deserve honesty and truth about your situation
- If your Partner doesn't stand by you while you Recover you are better off without them
- Children want your time with them, more than they want your wallet
- Parents worry – they cannot help it. Give them patience and understanding
- You MUST surround yourself with positive friends and stay away from negative conversation
- If you believe in God or a Greater Power, lean on them, let your faith be your friend

Finance

- It is going to be tough but achievable
- You may need to lean on your partner for a while
- Stay highly organised, even if you cannot pay bills, stay in control of your paperwork and budget
- Utility companies, banks and mortgage providers are more understanding than you expect
- You are going forward with Bouncepreneurs to become Rich. Not merely to survive

Fitness

- You need to be mentally strong and to do this you need to be fit
- You have to get the massive amount of stress out of your body, get very fit right now
- Fitness is not expensive. There are masses of totally free options, just go on Pinterest
- People around you will respect you more if you look fit and healthy
- Go clean, stop drinking, eat healthy food which is often cheaper
- Avoid vices which rob you of vitality and self-respect

Focus

- This is the time to be the most focussed you have ever been in your life
- Losing your own business may be a blessing in disguise - focus on that concept
- Focus on your own well-being you have nothing to prove to anyone else
- Make your administration of household and legacy business administration a tool of precision
- Focus on where you want to get to. Not where you've been. Happiness, wealth and fulfilment

Next we are going to take a detailed look at Entrepreneurial Grief. Which IS both <u>worse</u> and damages you <u>more</u> than losing your business!

3. You Have Entrepreneurial Grief

3.1. Entrepreneurial Grief What is it?

"Entrepreneurial Grief is a state of mind and physical health that entrepreneurs have relating to the feelings of loss they endure over being compelled to close a business. These feelings are highly tangible and some research suggests they equate to the loss of a loved one. "

Because entrepreneurship has been described as

"The ultimate stage for the demonstration of personal achievement."

Everyone can see that the entrepreneur's path is emotional, filled with passion, zeal and optimism, garnished with plenty of doubt and fear.

So if a business is lost, isn't a period of Grief understandable? Of course it is

Here comes a critical point from this book.

It seems that for most people it is the Grief phase that is <u>more</u> destructive than their <u>actual</u> business failure.

Not just in emotional BUT also in financial terms.

Entrepreneurial Grief is a state of limbo following the loss of a business. Very often the entrepreneur is suffering in many ways at this point. But for a successful recovery to be made, a short but MEANINGFUL transition through this Grief process is essential.

3.2. Goals of this Chapter

So there are four main learnings to come from this Chapter.

1. Understanding Entrepreneurial Grief fully (sharing real comments from those who have experienced it)

2. Getting through it as quickly as possible, but not so fast as to create a false recovery

3. Taking the Learnings from It

4. Moving On from Grief and leaving it firmly behind

According to Professor Dan Shepherd Entrepreneurs are recovered from Entrepreneurial Grief when

"His/her thoughts about the negative events surrounding and leading up to the loss of the business no longer generate a negative emotional response."

So helping "failed" entrepreneurs to reach this stage has to be my first objective and you the reader's goal. In this chapter we are going to explore (but not resolve – that comes next):-

- Exactly what is Entrepreneurial Grief?
- The Costs of Entrepreneurial Grief versus Your Actual Business Failure
- What to Expect During Your Own Entrepreneurial Grief Phase
- Ways People Suffer - Real Life Comments
- Allocation of Attention – the Killer in Entrepreneurial Grief
- And finally an exercise to help you

3.3. Understanding Entrepreneurial Grief

To reach a recovery, you first need to understand how you are being afflicted. So this chapter seeks to explain it fully. Then we move onto the solution.

If you do not understand and recover from Entrepreneurial Grief, you are looking at an extended period of misery. Let me assure you of that, speaking as one who knows.

Learning from failure is good, but emotional and traumatic experiences obstruct learning. So we seek to remove these experiences first.

We aim to help you make a complete and lasting recovery.

It is worth saying that research shows (Professor Deniz Ucbasaran) that achieving a full entrepreneurial recovery is easier if you are:-

- A Portfolio Entrepreneur who is used to successes and failures
- An Entrepreneur who has failed, but has known strong entrepreneurial success in the past.

But the hardest Entrepreneurial Recoveries are for 1st time entrepreneur who only know failure OR serial entrepreneurs who have endured more than one failure in a row.

I personally believe that long term Entrepreneurial Grief and poverty are the twin pestilences of our post credit crunch economy. Work by Professors Jonathan Levie and Mark Hart on the Global Entrepreneurship Monitor suggests that there can be a much, much higher reluctance to restart entrepreneurial activity after business failure in deprived areas, compared with affluent ones.

A vicious circle for sure.

If you are from a deprived background and have tried and failed to be an entrepreneur I really hope my guidance can work for you most of all. I have tried to picture a Bounce Back based on grim financial and debt realities and the need to cheaply yet thoroughly test your new venture to ensure it succeeds.

But this book most definitely seeks to offer assistance to all.

3.4. Entrepreneurial Grief Further Explained

There is evidence that the Grief is at its highest in the immediate aftermath of the business loss and typically lasts over 24 months. Couples can often suffer from this Grief jointly if they previously ran a business together.

However in some cases the Grief phase can last much longer and can be compounded by loss of esteem, income, financial stability and relationship breakdown.

Importantly the duration of the Entrepreneurial Grief can be reduced significantly with the introduction of intervention.

Entrepreneurial Grief is commonly confused with Fear of Failure. However they are entirely different from each other. Often Fear of Failure is given as a single reason why entrepreneurs find it difficult to move forward and out of entrepreneurial grief. But we will explore this in further depth later.

3.5. Manifestation of Entrepreneurial Grief

Entrepreneurial Grief manifests itself in five main ways or Costs of Failure. The one that towers above the others, due to practical urgency and it is of course Finances.

Five Faces of Entrepreneurial Grief

i. Finances – i.e. credit rating, cash
ii. Social Standing – whether it be real or self-imposed
iii. Physical – exhaustion, high blood pressure, insomnia, weight loss or weight gain
iv. Psychological – panic attacks, anxiety, phobias, paranoia and mood irregularities
v. Relationships – across a range of family members and friends

The physical and psychological costs of failure often, very often lead to depression which of course then leads to a loss of motivation.

As indicated earlier, if the entrepreneur has had success in the past, it is easier to recover. But the failure of a first business generates more grief.

The loss of a family business even harder, especially if second or third generation, is probably where the highest level of guilt driven Entrepreneurial Grief is felt.

It is worth remembering that a single failure is socially explainable as "just one of those things or an anomaly. But if a person has multiple failures and this is known publically, then loss of faith and ability to conquer adversity builds significantly, as this is much harder to explain away.

As we will explain in more detail shortly Grief can also interfere with your allocation of attention. For example dealing with bills. It also drives decision making (or lack of decision making) which is contrary to your interests.

Bouncepreneurs have told me that in Entrepreneurial Grief they often compounded their money problems by poor attention to the household finances. For example not paying a £35 parking fine, led to a later fine of £400 levied by a bailiff.

So Entrepreneurial Grief is very tangible. Let's now explore how it may be affecting you and preventing you from moving forward to success.

3.6. The Costs of Entrepreneurial Grief versus Your Actual Business Failure

People and experts talk a lot of business failure, they talk about start-ups too. And they talk about innovation. A favourite recently is Fear of Failure (FoF). But what you don't about is Entrepreneurial Grief.

Let's think about the personal financial impact on an individual.

During their last year of trading most business owners do draw an income. Sometimes reduced, sometimes drastically reduced, but they do draw a salary, even if it is staccato. But once the business has FAILED there is **no** salary. I repeat NO salary.

A sole trader can liquidate assets to generate cash, but a Director cannot do so once the business has gone into liquidation, as those assets belong to the creditors via the receiver. But the main thing again there is NO salary.

Now if the failed entrepreneur is a serial entrepreneur revenue from other business, she can pay her bills. The may even be a Black Kangaroo Bouncepreneur (more of this later) which prevents the loss of one venture being ruinous. But, if the business was the only source of revenue this person is in

<u>Worse Shape After the Business Fails Than Before!</u>

Now that is not going to make the front page news is it? But think about it. You have to pay your bills and you have no money.

AND you are in a state of grief.

So what do you do? You scramble around trying to find some money, normally by one of the following **EMERGENCY ACTION** means:-

- Scraping something valuable out of the failed business
- Get a full time job as soon as possible
- Get a temporary job just to put food on the table
- Borrow from banks or relatives
- Rely on your partner to support you
- Use savings (unlikely you have them if your business has been in decline)
- You sell assets – maybe your car.

All of these actions can be necessary. BUT

The longer your Entrepreneurial Grief goes on the more frantic your Emergency Actions will be and the more desperate you will become.

Put another way the damage you are doing to yourself in Entrepreneurial Grief is MORE destructive and MORE impactful than the loss of your business.

So your attention is on the wrong thing. You will be in Entrepreneurial Grief trying to function properly or in a depressed state.

Your ability to make sense of why the business folded and the social impact may be dominated you thinking and at the same time your self-esteem is very, very low.

So the key message here is this

<u>**Your Entrepreneurial Grief is Causing You More, Yes More Damage than the Loss of Your Business.**</u>

3.7. What to Expect During Your Own Entrepreneurial Grief Phase

The following lists are based on the Five Faces of Entrepreneurial Grief as mentioned earlier in this chapter. This conditions listed come from real people in four focus groups totally 48 entrepreneurs whose businesses failed in the UK. But they could have been anywhere in the world. I asked them to list what others should expect in this situation.

Some of the responses you would expect. Others are a little surprising.

A. Finances

Cash position – Not everyone suffered financially from the business failure. Serial entrepreneurs with multiple enterprises felt it less. But single business entrepreneurs all struggle. Not rock science really! Men and women both reported much harder personal spending restraints and a need to drastically cut back at home.

Credit rating – the credit rating of most individuals, especially those who were not in limited companies took a <u>huge beating</u> as a result of the loss of their business. Typically, items on finance had to be purchased on a partner's credit rather than their own.

Job Seeking - Highly experienced white collar entrepreneurs found it harder to get work than trained blue collar equivalents. There seems to be a much more ready market for people who can do electrical work, plumbers, joiners, cooks, coders, nurses, seamstresses or teachers than people who have done specialist business management roles. Often those with specialist trade skills were able to work of good rates of pay within a few days of losing their businesses.

On the other hand, those who had been working in leadership of owner-manager roles in consulting, project management, HR, marketing (except digital marketing) and even sales roles found getting <u>work very</u> challenging. There was often an expectation that getting an interim management role or a similar role to one they had had in the past would be straightforward and quick. The reality experienced was the opposite.

Debt Chasers - Being pursued over the phone or on the door step for unpaid bills was not a big issue for the first three months. However pressure started to build rapidly at the six months mark.

The universally accepted experience was that staying in communication with personal creditors was advisable, even when household bills or mortgages could not be paid.

Unexpected Costs – Unexpected charges and costs linked to their previous enterprise gave people unexpected and sometimes nasty surprises. This was notable where leased equipment was involved with the finance companies unwilling to accept returned equipment and coming after the business owner privately for the payments. Sometimes even after liquidation.

Failure to cancel small charges such as annual website domain renewal for example, would unexpectedly see money disappear from personal bank accounts. Often the business owner had a few small items running out of their personal account that they had simply not been concerned about as a business expense. But as a personal expense these charges bit into limited personal capital.

Cost of Money - The cost of borrowing money, bank accounts, credit cards and especially car finance all shot up when the business owner had lost their enterprise. Often the business had leased the owner a vehicle. Once able to get out of this contract (or the vehicle was simply taken back due to non- payment) the entrepreneur had to source an alternative on finance. At this point the low interest deals they had been familiar with in the past, were no longer available. Specialist finance companies with much higher interest rates were the only alternative. So not only was the individual driving a less sophisticated vehicle – they were paying more for it!

B. Social Standing

Real or self-imposed – firstly if a small business owner suffers the loss of their business it is not going to be announced on the 10 o'clock news let's face it. But entrepreneurs who had lost their business often state that at the time they felt all their neighbours knew and it was the "talk of the town." But later they tended to accept, in reality it wasn't.

The further down the path of entrepreneurial recovery people seem to go the less they see business failure as important to their social standing.

In Business Communities – in business communities your standing can really be badly affected if you get the wrong "blabber-mouth" competitor or e-zine announcing your troubles to the world. This is why Lifeboat companies in the same sector are not always a great idea. Several entrepreneurs reported that problems with competitors or general gossip, really hampered the success of their Lifeboat company and that too went down.

In Local Communities – The views regarding your local community standing seem to be linked to the type of place you live. Those living in metropolitan areas seemed to be far less affected by the impact in their local communities, largely because they didn't know people living around them too well. By contrast those living in small village communities were acutely affected by it.

Car – The biggest reason why most small companies fail is that they simply run out of cash. When this happens the leased/financed car is one of the first things to be repossessed, so the shiny car goes. This is clearly one of the worst recollections of the business failure. Having to climb from a bright shiny 5 series BMW into a banger, seems to one of the biggest humiliations an entrepreneur (female or male) can have.

Social Activity – "Failed entrepreneurs" cannot afford to go out as much. It is that simple. So they don't go to the wedding because they cannot afford the trip, or the gift or both. I know myself I had to miss the wedding of a trusted friend's daughter in Yorkshire. It pained me greatly. Presence in the local bar or club on a Saturday night is quickly missed. Or that trip to Marbella Spain for the hen party cannot be made, putting real pressure on friendships.

Pretty soon the old social life ceases to exist and this has added to the feeling of Grief felt by failed entrepreneurs.

C. Children

In all the elements of Entrepreneurial Grief, perhaps the most humbling and indeed sweet comments made by the focus group attendees was the attitude of their children. Wracked with guilt about not being the provider the wanted to be, Mum's and Dad's all had a similar message. It was this.

Children even the moody teens seemed to value more time with their parents doing simple things, like walking the dog, spending time chatting or playing games. Failed entrepreneurs often said they had to put on a "brave face" for their children. But those who sat down and explained the position with children, without alarming them, always got a positive response.

"My daughter was 15, stroppy and demanding in terms of the latest tech. Once we discussed the situation as a family, she got a weekend job and bought her next phone out of her own earnings. She was proud of herself and knew she had done well as a member of the family."

D. Physical

Exhaustion – Our group found wrapping up the business exhausting. The early days of having no business equally so. Everyone reported fatigue. Everybody.

High Blood Pressure – interestingly high blood pressure came through very strongly as a major physical effect of entrepreneurial grief. More than a few in our group had been to the doctor to see about blood pressure and palpitations

Insomnia – In the days leading up to business failure, insomnia was universal. That is to be expected. But despite a feeling of exhaustion, insomnia remained a problem for many people throughout their Entrepreneurial Grief phase. Insomnia was very prevalent amongst entrepreneurs who had lost their businesses some time ago.

Weight Loss or Weight Gain – It was surprising that weight gain was nowhere near as prevalent amongst those suffering entrepreneurial Grief as weight loss. Generally the focus group attendees were a skinny bunch. We heard a few accounts of how running or cycling had taken over their lives as a way of managing stress. We also heard how poverty had reduced the ability to buy and drink alcohol.

Dress – The group suggested that as Grief took hold, their personal appearance started to slip. They felt they had become less well-groomed or particular about their appearance. Several people spoke of working in their pyjamas all day long.

E. Psychological

Blame – Our 48 Entrepreneurs talked openly of their tendency to blame others for the failure of their business. There was clearly a spectrum of evolution in terms of recovery. Those who had reached the definition of Entrepreneurial Recovery outlined earlier,

"When his/her thoughts about the negative events surrounding and leading up to the loss of the business no longer generate a negative emotional response,"

Were not as likely to blame others. They tended to make statements such as

"When all is said and done I got it wrong"

"Because we had been working like that for years I didn't imagine we could be overhauled by a competitor so quickly, I just failed to react."

"The regulations came out and I ignored them. It was my bread and butter. Others invested in the training, I didn't!"

Panic Attacks – although not widespread, a few individuals admitted to suffering from panic attacks from the pressure.

Anxiety – knowing continuous anxiety about financial challenges and making decisions was a universal experience in the group.

"A horrible, horrible feeling that just would not go away"

"The anxiety in that first six months has shortened my life by 6 years."

"The anxiety of losing the business was bad enough, but fearing the next knock on the door for months was much worse."

Phobias – interestingly, fear of post and letters was widely cited by the group.

Paranoia – the Group showed a real mixture, with some members simply ranting about the role of their bank, or supplier, customer or even business partner who had caused their downfall.

There was anger over the way the State supports people who have lost their jobs or immigrants compared to long term successful entrepreneurs who had fallen on hard times.

Finally there was some resentment of London "this would not have happened if I had been in the South or London."

Anger – Some members of the group displayed a thin veneer of calm over the loss of their business. Just the lightest memory caused them to flare up in a state of clear anger over the circumstances.

A completely different area of anger came forward too. This was a tendency to rise to anger with loved ones for no real reason.

"In the early days, I took far too much out on my husband. The truth is he was a brick, supported me, and paid all the bills after the failure. One night, we were staying away for the night in a hotel. I got so angry because of his snoring….. He has always snored…. Then I stood up on the bed and kicked him so hard I thought I had broken his leg. I showed him no sympathy and let him sleep in the en-suite shower room. He limped for a week."

Faith – The tendency for Entrepreneurs to turn to faith in troubled times was clearly demonstrated by a number of comments. Although a belief in a God or higher power was not universal it was a majority held belief.

Typical comments included:-

- "My faith was revived over this period of Grief. I really leaned on it heavily in my darkest days"
- "Jesus was my rock and my shield"
- "I could hear my parents looking down and saying don't give up"
- "I believe in a force of good in the Universe and this seemed to look after me."

3.7.7. Relationships

<u>With Spouse or Long Term Partners</u>

Unfortunately the impact of Entrepreneurial Failure and Grief were not good.

Divorce - in our focus groups 7 delegates told us they were divorced or separated pending divorce and felt it was the pressure of the business that was mainly to blame.

Pulling together – 8 of the focus group members belonged to a couple that worked together. This group saw mutual understanding as beneficial, but that the relationship and recovery was problematic.

The observations of the focus group with longer term relationships will be revisited again when we look at Recovering from Entrepreneurial Grief.

<u>With Shorter Term Partners</u>

Again the impact of Failure and Grief on this type of relationship were not good either.

Most entrepreneurs with partners they had been seeing for less than a year had an experience of losing their relationship. Four of the six involved who had been in relationships for less than a year had lost their partner. Two-thirds and all men.

The lack of money available to go out with partners and also lying to the partner about the state of their finances and business were mentioned as the main reasons for the breakdown of the relationship.

There was clearly significant bitterness here which added to the Entrepreneurial Grief.

"She loved it when I had cash, but not so much when I didn't"

"I started to joke with her about finding a better boyfriend with more money, who could take her out more, one day she did!"

"To be fair she wasn't a bad girl, but my spirits were very low, I had no money and a better offer came along."

"What makes it so hard for me is that she never got the chance to see me as a success, so she only thinks of me as a Broken Man."

Children – we have already covered children and how resilient they are to Entrepreneurial Grief. But there were some heart breaking statements made in the group.

"I am a single parent mother and after the business failed I was drinking too much. I sent my twins to school without proper lunches, but bought myself a bottle of wine every night. I am so ashamed of that period."

"My daughter started doing accountancy at Uni. She has helped me get a better understanding of financial control and it has really brought us closer."

"No event in my life has upset me more than not being able to buy my kids a summer holiday."

"My six year old son came downstairs late one night for a drink. He put his head in my lap and said Daddy, I didn't like your stinky old office. Can you have a company where we make things and I can come after school?"

Parents – Three key concepts emerged regarding parents and their attitude towards Entrepreneurial Grief

   a. Parent's age seems to matter. Entrepreneurs tended not to discuss it with very elderly relatives, but would do with younger ones.
   b. Parents were the main source of borrowing when money was needed and there was both gratitude and shame in this
   c. In a minority of cases parents seemed to use the failure and low spirits of the Entrepreneur to suggest the whole of their entrepreneurial career had less validity that getting a "real job"

Friends –This is one of the hardest areas for those suffering Entrepreneurial Grief to see clearly.

The majority of the Research Group participants had SIGNIFICANTLY downsized their group of friends during the grief phase. There was also a marked resistance to spending time with people who "moaned about petty issues at work, in their nice secure job."

A widespread sentiment was along the lines of "you really find out who your friends are."

The other most common sentiments were stated in these ways.

- "Realising I was surrounded by some very negative people"
- "Feeling that friends in long term secure employment were alien to my world"
- "She seemed to be taking enjoyment from my fall from grace"
- "I opened up to one friend who proceeded to tell me everything I had done for 20 years was flawed. It was hard to take from a primary school teacher with zero entrepreneurial experience"
- "He quizzed me in depth about my situation after he'd dangled some badly needed work in his FTSE 500 company in front of me, then told me he never worked with friends and would refer me to a colleague but never did"
- "Be prepared for some surprises"
- "Those I expected to vanish because I did not have the money to play in their world didn't, moreover they opened doors and gave huge support"
- "They say you become the average of your five best friends. I had and it did not serve me at all well. But I've learnt from that and have a new set of friends now"

3.8. Allocation of Attention the Real Killer in Entrepreneurial Grief

3.8.1. How Long Does Recovery Take?

It might surprise readers to hear how long our Research Panel members took on average to recover from their own Entrepreneurial Grief. We used Professor Shepherd's definition as the yardstick.

On average 21 months.

No to be clear that does not mean these people had restarted a successful business, no. Some of these people had actually gone back to full time employment.

It took 21 months to effectively put the grief behind them.

If we take paying the mortgage as an example. Someone who has not paid the mortgage for 3 or 6 months is not going to be evicted from their home. But after 21 months? What do you think?

Someone who has been low for 3 months will get the love and support of a relatively new partner. But after 21 months, well they are going to leave aren't they? After all they have a life to lead and are entitled to happiness themselves.

And the Jobcentre or employment office. After 21 months of paying you unemployment benefit are they going to allow you to keep looking for that Director's or Senior Management role you believe you are skilled or experienced enough to do? No they are going to say you take that job down at the supermarket now because we are stopping your unemployment payments.

3.8.2. Harsh Realities

Entrepreneurial Grief plays on your Allocation of Attention. In effect it makes you look and go over events and thoughts that do not move you forward.

Instead of working on moving forward your attention is focused on:-

- What went wrong?
- Who failed you?
- Could Have, Would Have, And Should Have!
- What will the neighbours say?
- Tactical hand to hand financial trench warfare with creditors

3.9. Exercise

Below we have a Wheel of Life. Some of you may have completed something like this before. We have a second version of this in Chapter 5 so please complete it based on how you feel right now.

You need to decide for each segment how happy you currently are with your life. 1 being very unhappy and 10 very happy. There are some questions below the wheel to guide you.

Fill it in. If you feel you Money is non-existent you can shade in to 1 in the Money slice. For example, if you feel Family and Friends are a real strength fill this slice in to a 10. You will end up with a shaded area that clearly shows how you feel about your life right now.

Why do we ask you to do this after talking about Entrepreneurial Grief?

It is simple, you **will** see a realist view of your current position. But you will find positives to draw strength from. It might only be one or two segments. But you **will** see positives from which to build.

Secondly you will see things that have not served you well. So it may be time to let these things go. From this you may be able to see that change will improve your life and make you happier and maybe even MORE prosperous

YOUR WHEEL OF LIFE

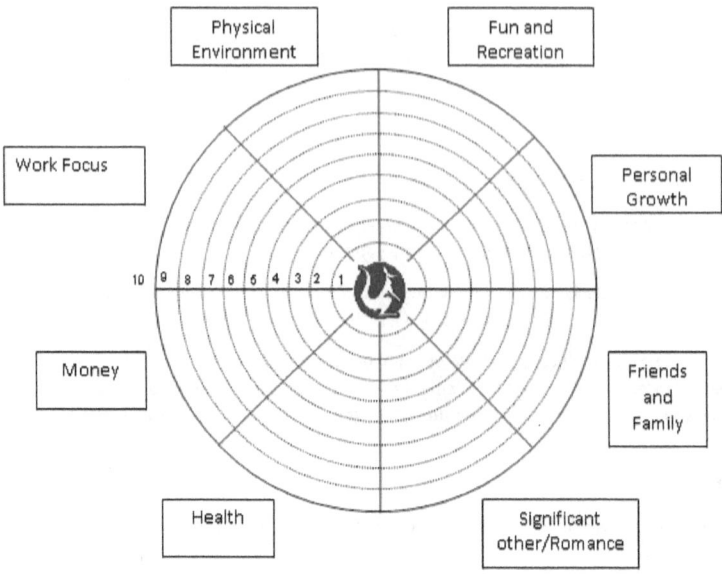

Work Focus

- Is what I do rewarding?
- Does my normal work reflect my values?

Money

- Did I earn enough and live within my means?
- Did I save enough?
- Was I planning for financial freedom?

Health

- Am I generally fit and well?
- Do I eat healthily?
- Do I exercise regularly?

Significant other/Romance

- Do I feel supported?
- Am I sharing values and intimacy?
- Am I nurturing a positive relationship

Friends and Family

- Do I feel supported by friends?
- Do I spend enough time with family and friends?
- Do I value the relationship we have with each other?

Personal Growth

- Am I always learning new things?
- Do I enjoy new opportunities for growth?
- Are the things I do growing me as a person?

Fun and Recreation

- Do I have fun often?
- Do I know how to relax?
- Do I enjoy sports or have hobbies?

Physical Environment

- Do I like the area in which I live?
- I my home what I want in terms of comfort?
- Is my car serviced, clean and reliable?

3.10 What we've learnt here

So now you understand Entrepreneurial Grief and have set your life into a little bit of context. You may have major challenges. But it is not all doom and gloom.

Lift Your Head Entrepreneur – It's Not Over Yet!

In the next chapter we look at How You Can Recover from Entrepreneurial Grief. I cannot promise you that you will not feel the pain of Entrepreneurial Grief at, but I believe I can get you through to the other side faster.

So let's Hop On Hey!

4 Recover from Entrepreneurial Grief and Start Your Bounce Back

4.1. Objective of this Chapter

The objective of this Chapter is to help you to recover from Entrepreneurial Grief. But I do not pretend to be a neurosurgeon, miracle worker, sage, guru or psychic. Far from it. But I can help you to

- Take from the grief process and your business failure learning which will build up your self-belief.
- Help you to "package" your failure in a Sense Making exercise and confine it to history
- Pinpoint the rewards of moving forward and those things you MUST clear out and leave behind
- Show a See Saw idea to mover your Entrepreneurial Recovery into Bounce Back

But I should like to start by being responsible. Some of you will decide to return to some form of entrepreneurialism after reading this book. For me this is a success. For I thrive on helping entrepreneurs recover back to success and happiness. It is my passion. I hope you will become a Bouncepreneur and Bounce Back successfully using the Kangaroo Bounce Back Plan later in this book.

4.2. There Are Alternative Pathways

But some readers will decide this is not the pathway for them, maybe not at the moment at least and choose other paths.

My prime objective is your happiness.

It is NOT to push you back into Entrepreneurial activity if this is not a path you choose to take, or are ready for.

Your happiness and well-being is my main concern.

So read this. But do remember there is more than one pathway to Entrepreneurial Recovery and they all deserve respect, these are:-

   a. Entrepreneurial Bounce Back – immediate return to entrepreneurial activity after healing from Entrepreneurial Grief.
   b. Hybrid Job/Entrepreneurial Bounce Back – Working to pay the core bills while starting a part time Entrepreneurial Bounce Back.
   c. Job – Full time job with no intention to return to Entrepreneurialism.
   d. Academic or Training Full Time – Academic career in teaching or further education AND/OR returning to full time training.
   e. Full Year Out in Charity or Travel – taking a year out to travel or do charity work as a means to rest and fully recharge before making any firm decisions on how to move forward.

4.3. How Entrepreneurial Failure and Grief You May Have Improved You

Make no doubt Entrepreneurial Failure will have changed you. But your Entrepreneurial Grief phase may have changed you more. If you are coming to this book following an extended period of Entrepreneurial Grief then you will have changed significantly in terms of confidence, fear of failure and decision making.

But the positive news is that many of the changes you will have undertaken will have had a positive impact on you as a person, a business person and an entrepreneur.

<u>Increased your human capital</u>

Your stock of knowledge, habits, creativity, social and personality attributes, will now be higher. This point is useful for you whether you enter the job market or return to entrepreneurship

<u>More considerate</u>

You will be more considerate towards others, especially others who are struggling in business. You will see clearly when business owners you know or work with, are facing challenging times. In fact you will develop a sixth sense in this.

<u>Higher level learning</u>

According to Professor Cope, this form of learning, is gained through EMERGING from entrepreneurial failure. But importantly this form of learning allows the returning entrepreneur to have a more evolved view of themselves in general.

<u>Greater desire to demonstrate competence</u>

The loss of a business, followed by transition through Entrepreneurial Grief leads to a much stronger desire to demonstrate competence. This desire may be rooted in pride, but it is positive due to the fact that it drives focus on skills and delivery.

<u>Greater attachment to the success of the venture</u>

Entrepreneurs in general know that association to multiple failed business ventures can damage their reputation and more importantly self-view. But as many returning entrepreneurs have said, getting the cash together to restart a business is far harder than their first start up and this creates greater attachment to success.

<u>Better financial control</u>

The one area most people restarting in entrepreneurial activity consistently say they are working on and will need to improve is financial control. Specifically using software regularly for financial control.

<u>Focus on demand sources</u>

Another commercial area, which improves is seeing demand. You will scrutinise temporary, fad or unstable customer demand far more closely than you perhaps did on your first time start up.

<u>Clearer business models</u>

There is some research that suggests and arguably criticises restarting entrepreneurs go for less innovative businesses than start-ups. Well you are not in the business of creating innovation statistics, but you are in business to make yourself rich. If your business models is simple in the extreme, then go for it. But follow other Bouncepreneurs in creating clearer business model in which to invest your future.

<u>See more opportunities</u>

You will be able to see more opportunities.

Learnt to grow less rapidly to maintain cash

You may seek to grow less quickly – especially if your earlier demise was due to cash flow failure. Whilst understandable, this is of course a "double-edged sword."

Risk averse

Risk will frighten you more. But not necessarily across all your thoughts, like a first time entrepreneur. Maybe your fears will be more selective.

Better decisions of viable business models

Once you have got over your Entrepreneurial Grief, you will make better decisions in terms of viable business models. You will look for simpler, repeatable and scalable business models.

Greater desire to understand long term sustainable demand

As a returning entrepreneur you will take the extra steps to fully understand the long term demand opportunity you are planning to base your future on.

4.4. What Rewards Does an Entrepreneurial Bounce Back Offer

Reward 1 – Happier

People become entrepreneurs for a broad number of reasons. Money is top of the list really. Successful rich entrepreneurs seem to be happy in most cases. I have never met one who is not.

So starting again and becoming a success WILL make you happier. Let's keep it as simple as that.

Reward 2 – A Better Business Model

Your earlier failure will grate on you if left unresolved. Research shows that those who go back to full time employment suffer for pangs of entrepreneurial grief for far longer than those who Bounce Back.

Reward 3 – Life Clear Out

Your business failure may be a real opportunity to clear out your life of people, habits, beliefs and self-doubts that have plagued your for years. See it as an opportunity for a renewal in your life.

Reward 4 – Richer

If you can convert the experiences you have taken from your business failure and convert them into wisdom, then you have the opportunity to make yourself rich.

This has to be your goal.

Your old business may have allowed you to pay your bills. But a job could do that couldn't it? So why did you endure the hardship of being a business owner.

It may even have allowed you to be comfortable for a while. To take some nice holidays, drive a nice car, wear nice clothes.

But you have lost your comfortable life style. It was a temporary arrangement.

The best way to lifelong security and comfort is real wealth. So this is your new goal.

"I just want enough to cover my bills," or "So long as I am comfortable" we it isn't going to cut it for you now is it?

Reward 5 – Give Back More

Once you are wealthy you can use you wealth and more importantly influence and ideas to help people reach out of poverty.

The lessons you have learnt you can share with young entrepreneurs and help to develop strong leaders as part of your process of giving back.

Finally the Bouncepreneurs Movement is a circular process. So as a result of moving forward in your own life you will be asked to assist others facing Entrepreneurial Failure and Grief in the future. This is your way of giving back more.

4.5. Sense Making Exercise

Sense Making can really assist your move out of Entrepreneurial Grief into Bounce Back.

Here is your exercise. What you need to do is to write a single short paragraph which explains to your own satisfaction why your enterprise failed. What you learnt from the experience and how it has made you a better person and entrepreneur.

Your story should be positive story.

- Truthful
- Ethical
- Show your core learnings

Some examples might be:-

"I ran my business with moderate but not consistent success for a number of years. I was proud of the employment I created and the exports I achieved. I now see that the business model lacked repeatability and scalability and this is a key feature I will insert into my future ventures."

"I really enjoyed running my earlier business, especially the interaction with my customers. I made some great friends. Unfortunately I did not see the threat of a poor stock control and financial management which gave me a poor understanding of my true cash position. I still understand the value of long term commitment to customers, but I will make sure I keep a close eye on financial control in my next enterprises."

"I know from my last venture that I am good at identifying opportunities before others do. I was able to dominate the market in this country very quickly. The thing I learnt was that I needed to internationalise business ideas and gain scale very quickly to become the market leader and to have long term security."

"In my last venture I showed that I can build a business idea into a working reality within 6 months. The key learning I took away from the experience was that I needed to delegate. I worked myself too hard and this led myself into poor health. But I have recovered fully and will take this experience into my next project."

"In my last business I took too big a risk on the ability of coding staff to deliver the software product we planned and missed our window of opportunity. I learnt that I myself needed stronger project management skills and ability to fully understand the work of my people."

Your Story Goes Here

_____
_____
_____

_____

Do keep this Sense Making statement handy. You will need it again shortly.

4.6. Entrepreneurial Grief versus Bounce Back See Saw

I want to give you an idea. You will have ups and downs, just like a see saw. But stay on the upside.

See Saw Up	See Saw Down
Your Business Failed not You	You/Your Business the same thing
Going Your Own Way	Needing Approval
Being Mindful and Moving Forward	Not Letting Your Past Go
Listening to Yourself	Listening to Society's Outdated View

You and Your Business Failure Are Not the Same Thing

It is essential you don't make your failure personal. You HAVE to separate the venture's failure from your own identity. You are not a failure simply because you have the right method or model to find great success. Your failure and your personality are not the same. If you make your failure about you, it will damage your will-power, clarity of thought and confidence. Even if your core value or relationships have been significantly troubled by the business failure this is not your identity.

Approval

Approval is a modern day pandemic. The use of social media for business and private worlds has led many to crave approval. Don't go down this road. This is vital. You may even look desperately for the approval of others about why our original business failed. People who have not walked a metre let alone a mile in your moccasins. You do not need the approval of others. Your self-esteem may have taken a real battering. But you do not need the approval of others. You really don't. Make you own decisions. Go you own way. If you give too much value and authority to the opinions of others your own fire could be extinguished. It is your life. Don't let anyone's approval block your road to success.

Do Let Your Past Go

What has happened to you in the past has happened. You cannot change it with Could Have, Should Have and Would Haves. Don't obsess over the failure it serves no useful purpose. Obsession of this kind will intensify the outcome, your Grief.

This is vicious circle of past thinking and lack of confidence. It stops you moving forward. These thoughts will be hard to set aside. But it can be done and you are going to do it!

We will come onto the idea of an entrepreneurial funeral shortly. But as you progress put this failure philosophy into daily use. Watch the Premier League or other top soccer teams.

The mind-set top players have is to give a short review of why things went wrong, work on putting them right and then moving on, putting failures where they belong. In the past!

Society is Backward on Entrepreneurial Failure

Society has a very unhealthy attitude towards failure. Take a look at LinkedIn or Facebook. How many people are posting news about their failures! None right! Try to change your perspective away from the negative and go for more productive and perspective view. A good idea is to stop using the term failure altogether and to use the terms learnings, a small but significant shift.

Mindfulness

One of the most useful ideas is to start thinking about your mental processes very differently. That voice inside your head, can you rely on it? Your mind can deliver success or failure. But deep down in your head there is a weathervane instinct telling you what to do. Not just what key decisions to make or business models to use. But also telling you things like:-

- When to put extra hours in and when to conserve your energy
- When to go to that trade show to learn something new
- Which new software you HAVE to learn

Don't listen to the first concept that jumps into your head. Wait and listen for that second weathervane voice of wisdom.

Imaginary Supporter

One idea to assist you is to create an imaginary partner. This partner relies on you to explain what happened to your failure. This method allows you to partially remove yourself form your emotions and to be objective in the analysis of your failure. Think about how you will apply this learning in your future projects.

4.7. Your Big Entrepreneurial Grief Clear Out

Right here we go. You already know you are facing several recovery barriers and every reader will have a different mix. Have a think about the list below and how they fit you.

Barrier 1 – Attitude

There are several attitudes, which although not too scientific represent barriers to a successful Bounce Back.

Zombie – you are in a Zombie like state, without clear direction, plan or idea of timescales. Don't be too hard on yourself. I understand, but you are not ready for renewed entrepreneurial activity.

Past Rather Than Future Focused – despite the fact your old business failed and caused you much Entrepreneurial Grief, you cannot let go of your "Glory Days."

Rose Tinted Spectacles – you are looking at past events in a false way. Many successful Bouncepreneurs have come to realise that their view of why their businesses failed evolved significantly in the years after failure. In fact a common comment is paraphrased as "I lied to myself as to why I really failed."

Mr/Mrs/Miss Angry – any discussion regarding the past business triggers an emotional outburst about "them" those who conspired against me.

Tough Guy/Tough Girl – this is a scenario where the Entrepreneur in Grief is in completely in denial about their state of mind and jumps aggressively into their next business without enough consideration. This seems to be very common in Life Boat restarts, where a failed business model is resurrected without legacy debt, but still a flawed business model.

Bull at a Gate – this attitude is similar to Tough Guy/Tough Girl but where a cavalier attitude to a new start exists and a VERY poorly conceived business model is attempted.

VIP Corporate Executive – Very common in white collar consultancy type restarts. Simply put the individual cannot shake off their view that they are still part of the business elite. They believe they have the right and more dangerously RESOURCES to rub shoulders and have the trappings of senior highly paid executives. This is sometimes manifested in the desperate desire to hold onto a car that simply cannot be afforded.

Too Much Time in the Pub/Bar or At Home – drinking too much affecting ALL decision making.

Jealousy – Not just envy but nasty jealousy of others (especially younger) who have done better and thrived in the entrepreneur's former business market.

None of these attitudes will help your entrepreneurial recovery!

Barrier 2 – Messy Finances

It is one thing to be short of money. But that is not the same as being badly organised with your finances. Be broke, but know who you owe money to and keep it closely monitored. Also keep in communication with those you owe money to.

You probably have 8 or fewer main domestic creditors. That is right 8!

You must have a clear picture of what your domestic costs are. Even if you are depressed and hiding under the duvet.

Are you the sole breadwinner? Or do you have a partner or other family members who could and SHOULD take up the slack? If you have been the breadwinner for years, insist on help!

What are your other revenues/savings and how are you able to eek these out until you restart.

Barrier 3 – Messy Relationships

If your personal life is in turmoil, perhaps divorce or simply not being stable at home, you need to really think hard.

Simply put, you need to know if you have the support both emotionally and maybe financially of your partner. If you don't you cannot easily recover from Entrepreneurial Grief and become happy and rich.

Barrier 4 – Poor Health

The first question is, can you fix your poor health yourself? Is it self-sabotage as a result of your Grief? If it is you need to work on your fitness. Get lots of sleep and eat right. If you are unfortunately suffering from a serious mental or physical health problem, you may need to work to pay your bills. Get a job until you are recovered enough to reconsider going it alone in the future. Treat yourself with care. Your priority is to get well first.

Barrier 5 – Addictions

Drinking too much, drugs, too much time on the internet. Seek help. Professional help. Recover well. Can you combine the recovery from an addiction with an Entrepreneurial Bounce Back?

Yes you can. People have done it. Find the strength. Confound your pundits. You are entitled to be happy and become rich. Don't let anyone say you cannot make it. Good luck to you.

Barrier 6 – Fear of Failure

Much has been written about Fear of Failure as a barrier to success. In fact I believe that government agencies and some academics are a little obsessed with it.

But their focus is on first time start-ups. Not on Bouncepreneurs.

But I would direct readers to the work of Professors Michell and Shepherd who argue that Fear of Failure is not a barrier to entry for Bounce Back. Their work has shown failure can drive greater effort, positively affecting the goal characteristics and goal pursuit.

Furthermore first time entrepreneurs have general Fear of Failure. But Bouncepreneurs have fear at different stages and more segmented fear levels. In short a more intelligent form of fear.

They also have more temporary fear and need less encouragement

Barrier 7- The People around You

We have all heard that you are the average of the five friends or five people you spend the most time with. This is most likely true.

It is essential that you surround yourself with people who can support you.

Your recovery is by no means assured. So you must ditch those people who drag you down in any of the following ways:-

Physically – boozy pub buddies

Positivity - Cynics "they" have got it in for us

Critics- anyone who pour destructive commentary on your plans or failure to get a job

Instead try to build a dream team of five Gurus/friends

- Fitness –someone to train with
- Mental Wellness – someone to talk to and share your troubles
- Love – someone who loves you as you are
- Accountant – someone who will improve you use of accounting software/financial understanding
- Fun – someone to have pure fun with

Barrier 8 – Your Worth in the Job Market

If you have been running your own business for a number of years you may find that your value to a corporate employer is not what you might think. Why?

Recruiters do not take risks – they want someone who has done the role before.

I have lost count of the times I have read adverts for roles like:-

- "You are already working in a similar role in a major enterprise"
- "You are used to working in matrix management systems"
- Must be able to demonstrate 3-5 years similar sales experience"

Other reasons you may not be able to find the job you want include:-

- Your experience may be too spread across sales, marketing, finance and operations.
- You may have not carried out a specialised role for some years
- Other candidates may have narrower and deeper experience/training which is more classically suited to the corporate world
- You may have been a big cheese in your own world, but your business has gone now
- Your credit rating may prevent you getting a role you might expect
- Recruiters think you may wish to return to self-employment and are just using them
- And of course that old classic "you are over-qualified."

Finally if you are thinking you will start a new business in 3-6 months, you might want to think about using your time looking for jobs to plan your new enterprise and paint houses, garden or anything else where you can make some money fast.

Washing windows and mowing lawns is a quicker way of generating money than trying to get an interim role – that's for sure.

Barrier 9 – You Have Nothing New to Learn

Your business failed. So there was something you didn't know!

In the UK we have a TV show. The Hotel Inspector. Alex Polizzi, (yes I have crush on her) the inspector gives failing hoteliers her expertise. The fact that corporations would pay thousands to get her in is wasted on some of these numskulls. These demi failures often resist the advice being offered even at the 11th hour.

They are too stubborn to learn of course. And my word, they look so stupid.

Don't be like that. You will need to re-educate. Not only do you need to be good at what you plan next. Your goal should be to be the most knowledgeable person in the WORLD in your field. Nothing less.

Barrier 10 – Fear of Becoming Rich

The Fear of being broke is bad enough. But why be afraid of getting rich?

Does it make any sense to you – becoming rich? Or does it just feel too far away from your reality right now? I can understand that feeling. I have had it myself

Either way you need to stop being afraid of getting rich.

DARE TO BELIEVE IT

Give yourself a happy life, invest in your loved ones and lastly don't put a buck in a charity box. You can help far more people if you are wealthy AND your views will be listened more than when you are broke!

If you decide to move forward and become a Bouncepreneur. You are doing it with the goal of becoming rich. Not to cover costs, neither to be comfortable.

You are doing it to become rich!

4.8. Entrepreneurial Funeral

Finally in this Chapter we would strongly recommend the idea of an Entrepreneurial Funeral for your Failed Business. This is something you can do with your close circle, or in a more organised format which is becoming more popular.

As an organised event, this idea is becoming very popular, originally starting in Mexico and now in multiple countries.

They usually involve three or four speakers taking to the stage to share personal, heart-rending stories of their deceased businesses. Some of these events are very melodramatic – sometimes there is even a coffin.

But not every small business owners wants to speak in a public event about their failure. You have a second option which is to focus more on your own loved ones and inner circle. Make it a dinner party, burn something outside connected to your failed business. Ham it up, get the kids involved. Make it a night to remember.

You are sharing what you want to share with those who are significant to you.

You can embed your sense making story (I told you it would be needed later) into the collective minds of your "Home Team."

If you are on your own. You can still do this. I suggest going to the supermarket buying something to toast with (if you are broke a cup of tea will do!), buy your favourite things to eat. Burn that memory item. Your old business cards or your logo emblazoned polo shirt. Your suit! Whatever it is burn it!

I strongly recommend that you do run a funeral or wake for your past enterprise. Lay it to rest once and for all.

You are drawing a line in the sand separating your past Entrepreneurial activity from your future

4.9. Summary and What's Coming Next

In this Chapter I have highlighted the benefits and rewards to making an Entrepreneurial Bounce Back, hopefully also helped you make sense of your earlier failures too. Making sure the things you must now leave behind has been strongly emphasised and I have suggested you hold an Entrepreneurial Funeral to bury the past Grief and to celebrate the Learning you are taking forward.

In the next Chapter we ask you to scrutinise yourself and to test your decision making before making a firm decision to follow the Kangaroo Guides into Bounce Back.

5 Are You Ready for a Bounce Back?

5.1. Introduction

Now it is time for you to take a close look at yourself and your readiness for a Bounce Back.

In this Chapter you have some work and hard thinking to do as we introduce the Kangaroo Bounce Back Assessment.

This Assessment is designed specifically to check your own position and to allow you to make the most informed decisions about what is best and realistic for you going forward.

By reading the previous chapters you will already be familiar with some of the assessment areas we want you to examine.

5.2. The Kangaroo Bounce Back Assessment is Not a Dream Crusher!

Because Bouncepreneurs always support a person who is trying to Bounce Back to Entrepreneurial Success, we never say you are not ready to try again.

We NEVER say this!

Why Not?

Because myself Michael Allen, other Bouncepreneurs, your girlfriend/wife or boyfriend/husband AND certainly not the world as a whole has ANY right to crush your dreams.

If you think you can Bounce Back go for it and our since message of good luck!

Please do come back and share your success with us on www.bouncepreneurs.com

This Assessment is designed to help you and your family to get the best possible route back to entrepreneurial or other success for YOUR specific situation.

I repeat FOR YOUR SPECIFIC SITUATION.

5.3. Now the Bouncepreneurs Name Makes Sense

When I have talked about this stage to people, they all say "Now I understand why you called the movement Bouncepreneurs!"

Kangaroos don't just bounce once do they? Actually kangaroos cross short distances in two or three small bounces, but man, when they get moving those bounces are huge. But they have the most efficient mode of propulsion in the animal world. THAT's A FACT!

But they always start with _small_ bounces.

Always!

So I want you to do the same.

Some of you may need just one bounce to get going to success and happiness.

Others may need two or even three bounces.

5.4. YOUR KANGAROO BOUNCEBACK AUDIT

Exercise Guidelines

Now we have a series of exercises for you. These are designed to help you decide which Bounce Back Pathway is right for you.

a. Bounce Back Readiness Self-Assessment Questionnaire
b. Plotting Your Bounce Back Readiness Wheel
c. Real Life Bouncepreneur Case Studies
d. Your Own Bounce Back Case Study
e. Making Your Bounce Back Pathway Decision

Bouncepreneur Self-Assessment

Firstly we will ask you to we will ask you a series of questions (described below).

Answer as honestly as possible. Don't be too hard or gentle on yourself. Be as realistic as possible. Your future success counts on it. It is important you do this entirely on your own. No one else needs to see your results.

A. Wellness

Grief. To what extent do you agree with the following statement "My thoughts about the negative events surrounding and leading up to the loss of my previous business no longer generate a negative emotional response in me." Tick the number box that best represents you	
I strongly agree, I feel zero grief	5
I agree and feel no real grief	4
I have the odd wobble, but mainly I agree	3
I disagree I have not let it go fully	2
I have to disagree as I still feel grief	1

Physical Fitness. Which of the following responses best describes your physical fitness at this point in time? Tick the number box that best represents you.	
I am in really good shape, with a regular fitness regime	5
I have been working on my fitness and am well on the way to getting fit	4
My fitness has slipped and I am not in good shape, but I can get it back quickly	3
I am pretty unhealthy at the moment	2
I have serious health problems I am wrestling with	1

Your Decision Making Ability. Which of the following responses best describes your ability to make decisions at this point in time? Tick the number box that best represents you.	
I am making clear strong decisions	5
Most of my decisions are clear and strong	4
Some of my decisions are good	3
I am still making poor decisions too often	2
I have trouble making any decisions	1

Rich Plan

Business Model. How confident are you in the success of the business model you are thinking about? Be very honest with yourself and tick the number box that best represents you.	
Very confident	5
Confident	4
Hopeful	3
Some concerns	2
Worried	1

My Next Business Finances. Which of the following best describes your ability to fund your next venture? Tick the number box that best represents you.	
I sufficient money to make a business investment	5
I have the ability to secure a loan for a new business	4
My business requires very small levels of money I do not need to borrow	3
I am not sure where I am going to fund my business from	2
I have not figured this out yet	1

Home

My Domestic Finances. How are your domestic finances? Tick the number box that best represents your situation.	
I have reserves and am relaxed about paying my bills for the next year	5
My partner is supporting me and I am relaxed about paying the bills for the next year	4
Things are tight but I or my partner and I can cover the bills	3
I don't have enough to cover my bills without a few car boots/online sales	2
Things are very tight and I am building up debts and not covering my bills	1

Your Life Partner or Spouse. Which of the following responses best describes your Partner's attitude to you trying self-employment again? Tick the number box that best represents you.	
My partner is fully behind my decision to try my own business again	5
I have the full support of my partner in what I wish to do	4
My partner does not agree with my plans but has agreed to support me	3
My partner does not agree with my plans and says they won't stand in my way.	2
My partner opposes my plans and pressures me to get a job	1

Skills

Financial Management Skills. Which of the following responses best describes your financial management skills at this time? Tick the number box that best represents you.	
I have exemplary financial management skills	5
I had a good control and knowledge of my business finances	4
My accounting skills are basic, so I am taking further education	3
I struggle with managing and organising accounts	2
I am dreadful at accounts and will have to rely on my accountant	1

Digital. Which of the following responses best describes your digital marketing and other digital skills? Tick the number box that best represents you.	
I am now highly skilled in this area	5
I have developed my skills to a good standard	4
I have some gaps in my knowledge which I am studying hard to fill	3
I am a lightweight in this area of my business	2
I don't think it is an important skill for me/I can hire someone to do this for me	1

Factory. How confident are you that you can make the product or service consistently well based on the resources and skills you have available to you? Tick the number box that best represents you.	
I am very confident now highly skilled in this area	5
I am confident	4
I am neither confident not unconfident	3
I am less than confident	2
I have significant challenges before I become confident	1

Well done on completing your Self-Assessment. Now one more task on it. Please revisit your questionnaire.

You have the ability to mark your assessment with 2 x Strengths (S) and 2 x Weaknesses (W). Just two mind! So now mark 2 Strengths (S) and 2 Weaknesses (W) on your questionnaire. Using the letters W and S.

Bounce Back Assessment Wheel

In the following Bounce Back Wheel you will see that one segment of the wheel corresponds to each of the question areas in your audit. If you score 3 on Digital Skills for example draw a line across the segment at the 3 point. Do this for each of the segment to get a really clear picture of how you sit on your readiness to make a successful Bounce Back.

Ask yourself these three questions:-

a. Is anything stopping me from making a Bounce Back as an entrepreneur?

b. What segments will I need to address before moving forward into Bounce Back?

c. Might I be better taking an alternative Pathway rather than a Full Bounce Back at this time?

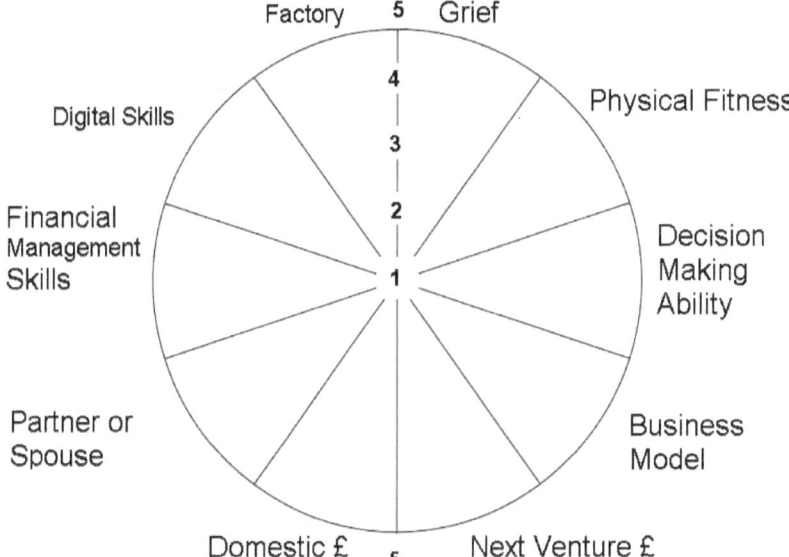

Bouncepreneur Case Studies Exercise

Explanation

There are now a series of real life cases studies (some details have been changed to protect confidentiality). Then we will ask you to take a look at a series of Bouncepreneur character profiles. These are based on real people who lost their businesses. It is always easier to assess others than yourself isn't it? But by stepping out of your own situation and looking at these other Bouncepreneurs you can better understand your own situation and how honest your being with yourself.

A. Please study them one by one.

For each case study write down what you think are the Strengths and Weaknesses.

Again you have a maximum of 2 x Strengths (S) and 2 x Weaknesses (W). But you do not have to use both. You can use 1 or none should you see fit.

Explain why you have awarded these Strengths and Weaknesses in a few of your own words.

B. Likely Success/Failure of an Immediate Bounce Back into a New Project

Next in a few of your own words write down what you think the likelihood of this person achieving success/failure will be IF they return to a new start up immediately. Give your reasons for this.

Also write down what needs to change for the person to move forward to more guaranteed success.

C. Best Recovery Route for Each of the Case Studies

Finally under each case study record which of the following represents the Recovery Route for each of the case studies and why in a few of your own words.

Remember the choices are:

- Entrepreneurial Bounce Back – immediate return to entrepreneurial activity after healing from Entrepreneurial Grief.
- Hybrid Job/Entrepreneurial Bounce Back – Working to pay the core bills while starting a part time Entrepreneurial Bounce back.
- Job – Full time job with no intention to return to Entrepreneurialism.
- Training Full Time – Training full time with a later return to entrepreneurial activity once new skills are gained.
- Full Year Out in Charity or Travel – taking a year out to travel or do charity work as a means to rest and fully recharge before making any firm decisions on how to move forward.

Here is a blank example of the Bounce Back answers you will be asked to complete on the following Bouncepreneurs.

Example Only Case Study Assessment – Jo Bloggs		
	Strength/Weakness	Why Do You Think This?
Strengths		
Weaknesses		
Immediate Bounce Back	Likely Success/Failure	
	Success or Failure	Why?
		What (if anything needs to change?)
Best Recovery Route	Select 1 Response Entrepreneurial Bounce Back [ ] Hybrid Job/Entrepreneurial Bounce Back [ ] Job [ ] Training Full Time [ ] Full Year Out in Charity or Travel [ ]	
	Why this Route?	

Person	Luc		Project	Copier Sales Business
Luc ran a photocopying business since the mid 1990's. Falling sales led to the closure of his business under pressure from creditors. Luc plans to restart this business as a life boat company.					
Wellness			Home	
Grief	Very socially sensitive to earlier failure	Domestic Finance	No income of his own, totally reliant on a partner he met 6 months ago
Physical	Drinking a little too much, poor fitness	Partner	Not supportive and prefer Luc gets a job
Decision Making	Strong but impulsive	**Skills**	
Rich Plan		Accounting	Good accounting skills
Timing	Poor, photocopier market has reduced significantly	Digital	No digital marketing skills at all
Bus finance	No new capital, but still owns 50 copiers which Mark believes he can sell	Factory	Copiers bought in from manufacturers

Case Study Assessment Luc		
	Strength/Weakness	Why Do You Think This?
Strengths		
Weaknesses		
Immediate Bounce Back	Likely Success/Failure	
	Success or Failure Why?	
		What (if anything needs to change?)
Best Recovery Route	Select 1 Response Entrepreneurial Bounce Back [ ] Hybrid Job/Entrepreneurial Bounce Back [ ] Job [ ] Training Full Time [ ] Full Year Out in Charity or Travel [ ]	
	Why this Route?	

Person	Anna		Project	Coffee Shop
Anna ran a cleaning company. Struggled to get reliable staff and ended up doing a huge amount of work herself. Exhausted she had to leave the business. Having seen a friend open a very successful and stylish coffee shop back in Portugal Anna saw an opportunity to repeat the model.					
Wellness			Home	

Grief	Moved on, but learnt importance of delegation	Domestic Finance	No additional income
Physical	Very fit, hobby triathlon	Partner	Supportive husband who is fully behind Anna
Decision Making	Strong	**Skills**	
Rich Plan		Accounting	Good accounting skills
Timing	Fair, Anna will not have the first coffee shop in the area	Digital	No digital marketing skills at all
Bus finance	Has savings of £20,000	Factory	Worked in coffee shops and familiar with preparation, hygiene & baking

Case Study Assessment Anna			
	Strength/Weakness	Why Do You Think This?	
Strengths			
Weaknesses			
Immediate Bounce Back	Likely Success/Failure		
	Success or Failure Why?		
		What (if anything needs to change?)	
Best Recovery Route	Select 1 Response Entrepreneurial Bounce Back [ ] Hybrid Job/Entrepreneurial Bounce Back [ ] Job [ ] Training Full Time [ ] Full Year Out in Charity or Travel [ ]		
	Why this Route?		

Person	Stefano	Project	Boat Building

Italian Stefano inherited a boat building business from his father. He launched a radical new boat concept which led the company into receivership. Independently wealthy, resilient Stefano decided to start again, planning to licence successful designs to boatyards globally.

Wellness		**Home**	
Grief	Highly resilient, glad to get out of the operational elements	Domestic Finance	Independently wealthy
Physical	Good fitness, competitive sailor	Partner	Long term girlfriend who lives in another country sees once a month
Decision Making	Confident	**Skills**	

Rich Plan			Accounting	Over-dependent on company accountant
Timing	Good, opportunities in expanding economies		Digital	Strong CAD design skills and boat design presentations
Bus finance	Selling concepts rather than boat building. Adequate finance from own resources		Factory	20+ years of working in boat production. MSC in marine engineering. Very knowledgeable
Case Study Assessment Stefano				
	Strength/Weakness	Why Do You Think This?		
Strengths				
Weaknesses				
Immediate Bounce Back	Likely Success/Failure			
	Success or Failure Why?			
		What (if anything needs to change?)		
Best Recovery Route	Select 1 Response Entrepreneurial Bounce Back [ ] Hybrid Job/Entrepreneurial Bounce Back [ ] Job [ ] Training Full Time [ ] Full Year Out in Charity or Travel [ ]			
	Why this Route?			
Person	Priya		Project	Fireplace Manufacturer
Priya had run a hair dressing salon. It paid the bills, but increased competition made it increasingly difficult. A decision by her landlord to change the property into apartments meant Priya had to close her salon. Finding out that a local manufacturer had closed, led Priya to buy the manufacturing equipment from the receiver for £15,000.				
Wellness			Home	
Grief	Upset to lose her salon, as her clients were also her friends. But learnt her business model would never make her rich.		Domestic Finance	Not in debt and can make some money as a mobile hair dresser to cover her personal outgoings. Ex-husband pays maintenance.
Physical	Not in great condition, starting to swim regularly		Partner	Divorced with two children. Single. Lonely & wants a relationship.
Decision Making	Not entirely confident		Skills	
Rich Plan			Accounting	Competent diligent book keeper
Timing	Competitive market but growing.		Digital	No knowledge of digital marketing

Bus finance	Used all her savings to buy equipment from receiver	Factory	No knowledge of making fireplaces. Hoping an employee can make them
Case Study Assessment Priya			
	Strength/Weakness	Why Do You Think This?	
Strengths			
Weaknesses			
Immediate Bounce Back	Likely Success/Failure		
	Success or Failure Why?		
		What (if anything needs to change?)	
Best Recovery Route	Select 1 Response Entrepreneurial Bounce Back [ ] Hybrid Job/Entrepreneurial Bounce Back [ ] Job [ ] Training Full Time [ ] Full Year Out in Charity or Travel [ ]		
	Why this Route?		

Person	Franz	Project	Turn Key Lodges

Franz lost his earlier business which was a camping holiday park. A bitter divorce, problems with alcohol and problems with unpaid business taxes led to a forced closure of the business. After two years working in Dubai in property sales and gaining control of his alcoholism Franz returned to the UK with a plan to sell holiday lodges to distressed camp sites.

Wellness		Home	
Grief	Overcome bad times well and reformed alcoholic. Knows the holiday camp business very well.	Domestic Finance	Has cash reserves ample to allow him to live without additional income for a year
Physical	Competitive triathlete	Partner	Single, with two estranged adult children
Decision Making	Very confident, clear plans	Skills	
Rich Plan		Accounting	Competent book keeper
Timing	Large number of potential partners needing additional revenue streams	Digital	Able to build strong digital presentations and understands WordPress and hosting well.
Bus finance	Has turnkey finance from Dubai investors	Factory	Agreement with turnkey building company
Case Study Assessment Franz			
	Strength/Weakness	Why Do You Think This?	
Strengths			
Weaknesses			

Immediate Bounce Back	Likely Success/Failure		
	Success or Failure Why?		
		What (if anything needs to change?)	
Best Recovery Route	Select 1 Response Entrepreneurial Bounce Back [ ] Hybrid Job/Entrepreneurial Bounce Back [ ] Job [ ] Training Full Time [ ] Full Year Out in Charity or Travel [ ]		
	Why this Route?		

Person	Petra		Project	Marketing Agency

Petra lost her Marketing Agency after being in business for 20 years. Focusing on traditional marketing without being able to deliver digital services was her downfall. Over-dependent on one key contract when this was lost the business became untenable and Petra closed. She suffered from serious grief compounded by the breakdown of her marriage. Plans to start a travel blog.

Wellness		Home	
Grief	Does not enjoy digital media, realises this fact.	Domestic Finance	Sale of house created some income which Petra has banked
Physical	Heavy smoker & very unfit	Partner	Bitter divorce still weighing heavily on Petra's mind
Decision Making	Not able to take major decisions	Skills	
Rich Plan		Accounting	Competent book keeper
Timing	Not the first travel blog.	Digital	Not great digital skills, plans to contract design for a blog site build.
Bus finance	Has income from house sale low start-up costs	Factory	Good copy writing skills and strong creative writing skills

Case Study Assessment Petra

	Strength/Weakness	Why Do You Think This?
Strengths		
Weaknesses		

Immediate Bounce Back	Likely Success/Failure	
	Success or Failure Why?	
		What (if anything needs to change?)

Best Recovery Route	Select 1 Response Entrepreneurial Bounce Back [ ] Hybrid Job/Entrepreneurial Bounce Back [ ] Job [ ] Training Full Time [ ] Full Year Out in Charity or Travel [ ]	
	Why this Route?	

Your Own Self-Assessment

Now complete a Case Study on You. Do it on your own and be honest with yourself.

Person	Your Name	Project	
Grief Recovery Statement			
Wellness		**Home**	
Grief		Domestic Finance	
Physical		Partner	
Decision Making		**Skills**	
Rich Plan		Accounting	
Timing		Digital	
Bus finance		Factory	
Case Study Assessment You			
	Strength/Weakness	Why Do You Think This?	
Strengths			
Weaknesses			
Immediate Bounce Back	Likely Success/Failure		
	Success or Failure Why?		
		What (if anything needs to change?)	
Best Recovery Route	Select 1 Response Entrepreneurial Bounce Back [ ] Hybrid Job/Entrepreneurial Bounce Back [ ] Job [ ] Training Full Time [ ] Full Year Out in Charity or Travel [ ]		
	Why this Route?		

There is a Road Map for everyone.

By doing the following assessment you have better determined the best route for your own recovery.

Remember the five routes we have mentioned earlier.

Now which one of these do you NOW feel is best for you right now?

1) Entrepreneurial Bounce Back – immediate return to entrepreneurial activity after healing from Entrepreneurial Grief.
2) Hybrid Job/Entrepreneurial Bounce Back – Working to pay the core bills while starting a part time Entrepreneurial Bounce Back.
3) Job – Full time job with no intention to return to Entrepreneurialism.
4) Academic or Training Full Time – Academic career in teaching or further education AND/OR returning to full time training.
5) Full Year Out in Charity or Travel – taking a year out to travel or do charity work as a means to rest and fully recharge before making any firm decisions on how to move forward.

As you know Bouncepreneurs is about bringing Entrepreneurs back to full success and happiness. So if your desire IS to return to entrepreneurialism, but you may not quite be ready then consider a staged recovery plan.

Also bear in mind in the Kangaroo Bounce Back Plan Black Belt Stage the Recovered Entrepreneur will be working on several businesses and is not married or emotionally bonded to any of them!

So your first Bounce Back could be a very, very modest business indeed.

Recovery Decision

We would now ask you to consider which is better for you. What suits YOU best?

None of these approaches are less good than each other. Just different.

1 Bounce Recovery – you simply bounce straight back into a new entrepreneurial business full time and full steam ahead.

2 Bounce Back- is where you move forward with an interim business or job, then go fully into entrepreneurship again.

3 Stage Bounce Back - is when you take time out to retrain or freshen up your mind and or skills, then try your Bounce Back.

Now I would like you to further build on your Sensemaking Statement that you made in the earlier Chapter.

Explain in fewer than 100 words your own Bounce Back Recovery Statement. Include

a. Which Recovery Route you have chosen
b. What you have learnt from the failure experience and will carry forward
c. What strengths you now have you didn't have before
d. Your biggest challenge and the impact is has on your decision making
e. Why you have made this decision

<u>Here are some examples to help you form your own statement</u>

"I have decided to go back into a **Full Entrepreneurial Bounce Back**. In my last venture I showed that I can build a business idea into a working reality within 6 months. The strength I now have is key learning I took away from the experience was that I needed to delegate. Now I have zero working capital and borrowing ability. So I will need to lean heavily on my partner for financial support in the planning and first month of this new business launch. I have made this decision because I believe I have a strong product idea and the ability to get revenue flowing quickly."

"I have decided to **Take a Year Out and Travel**. In my last venture I really felt exhausted. Although I have the germ of an idea for a new business I do not think I am fresh enough to pursue it. The new strength I now have, is that I no longer feel I know it all. I have had the arrogance shaved off me. I understand that I have to develop some new skills to ensure I am successful in future. I can study these during my break. My biggest challenge is my state of mind, I really feel tired and need to recharge for more than a two week holiday. I am fortunate that I have no children and am single. I can take off when I like."

"I have decided to get a **Full Time Job**. In my last venture I learnt that I am a natural in digital marketing, largely self-taught. But my ability to separate my hobby which I loved from a real business is very suspect. I did a crazy project and lost a lot of money. My new strength is commercial realism. But right now I have maintenance to pay for my daughter no money at all. None. So I must cover that expense and stop the bailiff coming to my door. The only way I can see this happening right now is to find a full time job."

"I have decided to relaunch my old business as seriously overhauled Lifeboat Company. But also to get a job. So it is a **Hybrid Bounce Back** for me. In my last venture I learnt that as a supplier I must pursue debts and not over-extend the range of products I was stocking. My new strength is understanding Stock Keeping Units and book keeping which I have studied hard. But I have debts which HAVE to be paid and my friend has offered me a 9-5 job in his company to help her for a year. So I will earn a salary and keep trading with my old business on the profitable lines. My plan is to go full time again in 12 months."

Your Statement

_____
_____
_____
_____
_____

5.5. Bounce Back Decision

You will know that many Christians believe in the concept of being born again, but a renewal of faith is something experienced in many other religions too.

Often people become born again because they really are sick and tired of being unhappy and may even feel that they have become a bad person.

As an entrepreneur whose business has failed, maybe your first start up, family business or other small business you have come to this book because you are very unhappy, saddened by loss, frustrated and feeling beaten down by failure.

Now it is time for an Entrepreneurial Resurrection and a Clean Slate.

If you feel that long term employment, time out travelling or education is the pathway for you right now, then good luck and hope to see you back in entrepreneurialism in the future.

There is no big speech here about only the tough keep going, or you've hit the wall and only the toughest, bravest, toughest, bravest, toughest bravest Bounce Back.

It may not be time for you to Bounce Back yet. But do Bounce Back in entrepreneurialism. Research does show that those who do not try again in entrepreneurial activity actually have the longest and deepest grieving process of all. Plus running your own show, becoming rich and happy – well it is such a worthy goal don't you think?

But for now why don't you say to those not quite ready to Bounce Back See Again Soon, Hasta La Vista and Auf Wiedersehen rather than Goodbye.

But if you have decide to become a Bouncepreneur from here on it is all about Bounce Back. You are going to be entering your Kangaroo Guide Phase.

5.6. Amateur versus Professional Entrepreneurs

Out there in Businessland we have Amateur entrepreneurs and Professional ones. To reach our goals of being a Rich and Happy Bouncepreneur only the Professional Entrepreneur approach will do.

You know we have all been Amateur Entrepreneurs to this point. Haven't we?

- We have planned badly
- Been casual in management
- Winged It
- Survived on lucky breaks
- Prayed to land one big deal to keep the ship afloat
- Used the VAT to cover cash flow

- Tried to find a partner with bigger pockets than wits

Well that ends now. Now you are a Professional Entrepreneur.

From here on you will walk, talk and believe you are a Professional Entrepreneur. You will treat every aspect of your business like a Pro.

- Brand new ambition
- Brand new clarity
- Brand new work ethic
- Brand new hunger for success
- Brand new goals
- Brand new purpose
- Brand new discipline
- Brand new decisions

If you get your head into being a Professional Entrepreneur then you will become an Advancing Woman or Advancing Man. No more Broken Men or Broken Women. People will see it in you. I promise you.

People around you will say

- "I have never seen a person change so drastically,"
- "What the hell happened to change her so much,"
- "I walked straight past him, didn't even recognise him,"
- "Her eyes are so steely now, clear determination."

You will attract people who want to better their lives and you will have no tolerance for the doom and gloom brigade.

In short people will see that you have been to "Hell and Back" and are not going back there EVER AGAIN.

5.7. Your Change in Mind Set

Bouncing Back means that you change your whole approach.

- You plan for success
- You test everything you do SO thoroughly before investing time and money
- You systemise your business
- You totally shun the need for approval
- You ignore the way HugeCorp do things or how consultant say it should be done

Why….. because you are so tired and fed up of failure, of playing small business, wasting time on crappy work and you are ready to take full control and responsibility for your actions in creating a Rich and Happy Future.

5.8. One Last Reminder

We are here to build your PERSONAL net worth. The money is your personal bank account, not the business. You do not need to fall in love with your next business idea. But it must work! You will have more than one business, you will become a Portfolio Entrepreneur.

Your businesses are there as Money Factories, from which you can extract wealth and do good things for your fellow human beings.

Remember we want Scale Up, Duplicate and Get Out Of (SDG) to be able to get out of the operation within 6 months.

5.9. Quick Final Alignment

As you are now a Professional Entrepreneur we are going to test your idea thoroughly. Very thoroughly.

We will check you can do all three of these things with it

- Scale Up
- Duplicate
- Get Out Of

We will also make sure it is not JUST going to cover your bills and NOT just going to make you comfortable.

Summary

In this Chapter you have taken a very deliberate consideration of your readiness to Bounce Back into entrepreneurialism. You've looked at 10 major states that will affect your readiness. You've also seen real life case studies of entrepreneurs whose ventures have failed, put yourself in their shoes and made objective decisions about readiness to go forward.

Then finally you have taken this challenging audit and put it into a final Kangaroo Bounce Back Assessment of your own readiness.

For those of you have decided a Bounce Back is the route for you, let's meet your new mentors

The 7 Kangaroo Bounce Back Guides to Success and Happiness.

Part 2 Kangaroo Guides to Your Bounce Back

Who to Expect

In Part 2 of this book you will meet a series of 7 Kangaroo Guides.

Each of these Guides will mentor you forward to a successful Bounce Back to prosperity and happiness.

The Kangaroo Guides are your loyalist of supporters. They are willing you to succeed. Each one has a different message for you to absorb.

Each one of your Guides wears a Karate Belt which they will give to you a belt to signify your stage of learning.

The belts run White –Yellow –Orange – Green – Blue – Brown – Black

At the Kangaroo Black Belt stage you will have successful achieved a full Entrepreneurial Bounce Back and this is something to be respected at the highest level.

Of course as you meet other Bouncepreneurs you will be able to discuss your recovery in common language based on your own stage of development.

If the venture you have in mind at the beginning of the process starts to look like a bad idea, which discovering can be a very good thing! You can go back to earlier Kangaroo mentors and restart the process at an earlier stage. I really encourage this process and it should NOT be seen as anything but a good thing.

What to Expect

There are three main things to expect from the second part of the Bouncepreneurs Book

1. Expect a very unconventional approach to running your next start up
2. See an extremely thorough idea testing process
3. Expect me to rid you of many of the lessons you have been taught about business

My default student is the penniless Bouncepreneur and to seek to help this individual at every turn

Why Kangaroos?

Kangaroos always move forward – they cannot go backwards! FACT!

They are inquisitive but do not embark on a long journey without careful inspection of conditions

Kangaroos know Dingoes (wild dogs) are dangerous but can handle them

Once Kangaroos get moving they are THE most efficient motion of all land creatures

6 White Kangaroo Blanching Your Mind For Bounce Back

6.1. Introduction

Your first Kangaroo Guide is the White Kangaroo. He wears long dazzling white robes. He has the air of complete calm about him. Totally calm and relaxed.

To <u>blanch</u> something is to transform it and make it suitable for the next stage. In the kitchen chefs will blanch an item to remove bitterness. You must do the same with your bad business memories

White Kangaroo's task is to prepare you for what is to follow. His personality is very different from any business guides or advisors you may have listened to in the past. He is 100% supportive of new Bouncepreneurs and really wants to see them Bounce Back to prosperity and success.

In this Chapter White Kangaroo is going to blanch some of the beliefs, experiences and thinking to give you a sharper edge to take on your Bounce Back.

White Kangaroo is often told to tone down this blanching process. But he believes too much advice out there comes from those who have never faced entrepreneurial failure. He is a really stubborn character with strong beliefs and he pulls no punches.

White Kangaroo gives you a no-nonsense approach. He makes no apologies for shooting dirty great big cannon balls into the established way of doing things.

6.2. Now it is Time to Let Go

You've looked at your Grief and White Kangaroo knows that this book has already taken you forward and put you in a better place.

Now it is time to leave all the gunk and rubbish blocking your route to entrepreneurial Bounce Back.

White Kangaroo wants you to write the date and time in the margin next to this book. The date and time you started your Bounce Back.

This is the time you are leaving your Entrepreneurial Grief behind once and for all.

You're the new butterfly emerging from the ugly cocoon.

Now White Kangaroo is going to kill off some sacred cows, corporate nonsense and plain babble which will interfere with your entrepreneur success.

The key message is, now it is the time to let go. Right now.

6.3. Approval and Attention

You don't need the approval of others OK. You don't!

White Kangaroo would like you to read this great quote to **set your mood.**

"Never surrender your hopes and dreams to the fateful limitations others have placed on their own lives.

The vision of your true destiny does not reside within the blinkered outlook of the naysayers and doom prophets. Judge not by their words, but accept advice based on the evidence of actual results. Do not be surprised should you find a complete absence of anything mystical or miraculous in the manifested reality of those who are so eager to advise you.

Friends and family who suffer the lack of abundance joy, love, fulfilment and prosperity in their own lives really have no business imposing their self-limiting beliefs on your reality experience."

Anton St.Maarten

Social Media - In this time of social media, there is a global epidemic of approval seeking. A worldwide obsession with it.

This is a big deal for people starting and especially restarting in business. It has emerged in all our focus groups and commonly crops up in meetings with your fellow Bouncepreneurs.

You will need to make <u>your own</u> path, make your own judgements and take decisions right for you which other people might not like.

Do not have a burning desire for the venture you are embarking on to be approved by those who:-

- Have no stake in your business as customer or supplier
- Should be supporting you anyway
- Have no experience in the area they are talking about
- May not have your best interests at heart

In fact if you are going to be a successful Bouncepreneur you need to let the desire for the approval of others go.

Why is it Vital to Let It Go? - Seeking approval will make you compromise your gut instincts says White Kangaroo.

It really will. If you feel you have a business idea that will work, check your own facts, do your own business analysis. If once you do this you feel it is a solid course of action – go for it. No one else needs to give you approval or validation. That's a mug's game.

The Needs of Your Situation May Far Exceed Your Need for Instant Approval – White Kangaroo tells an old Aboriginal story about a father and his daughter. Asleep by the fire, a snake enters the daughter's mouth. Seeing this her father jumps up and begin shaking her. He lifts her from the ground and shakes her violently, slapping and beating her body to dislodge the venomous snake.

The rest of the tribe look on in horror, cursing the man for beating his little daughter. Other men start to intervene punching the man to the ground. Every time he got back to his feet and continued shaking and slapping his own daughter, the other men beat him more and more viciously. Finally after receiving many blows from the other men of the village the snake finally emerged from his daughter's mouth and slid away. His daughter was saved and both she and the rest of the village instantly knew her "daughter beating" father was in fact her saviour.

The morale of this story is clear, you will have to forget the approval of others in order to meet the needs of your situation as a Bouncepreneur. This may go for your partner, your parents, and your family.

Disapproval Can Unsettle and Unnerve You - Focus on your own direction, what you think and what you are trying to do.

Remember disapproval is actually an empty bag. But some people use it as a weapon.

White Kangaroo reminds us we have all had our confidence knocked by a business failure, but you must NOT allow disapproval to derail you. Remember it is a "blank bullet" it can do you no harm. When you let people disapprove of you and cease to care, then your personal confidence will soar.

Don't be frightened to Disapprove of Disapprovers When I was starting Bouncepreneurs I had a lot of disapproval for my Kangaroo logo. A lot!

Things disapprovers said were:-

"It's like bounced payments"…. "It is too Australian" …… "Hard to spell"….. "Why blue?"…. "Why black?"…. "It's like Six Sigma"….. "Why not Tigger instead"…..

I heard them all. But the logo was free, I was broke, I liked it. It was a way to take the branding forward.

So when anyone tries to criticise my logo now I thank them politely and ask:-

"Where did you gain this terrific branding experience?"

"I don't think you've lost a business so it you won't get it!"

"I am sorry but I wasn't asking!"

That logo has become my talisman, my rock and I love it dearly.

Beware of Pack Mentality - Cults like the Nazis show us the power of peer pressure. Another good example was the Millennium Bug. Sometimes even in a small community or group of friends a leader emerges and believes they can decide like a Monarch what is acceptable and what is not. Followers often follow that leader blindly out of fear of exclusion or often just habit. They follow to comply with ridiculous levels so as to maintain the good favour of that leader and stay within the boundaries of the cult.

This happens far more in everyday life than we realise.

But it is essential you follow what you believe to be right, rather than what peer pressure may lead you to do. Stay true to yourself. And your own business plan of course!

You can't control what others think anyway - When you anxiously seek approval, you are really trying to hold onto control. Chances are in your business past you have seen your control slide away. So it is natural maintaining it becomes important. But controlling your Bounce Back is not the same as controlling what others think of you. Is it?

Simply put, you cannot control what others think so why bother trying!

Practice saying what you think - Once a day say something based on what you think and not what you think is going to be a crowd pleaser. It is fun. Get used to stating your own views in a straightforward way. Practice this and your views will gather increasing gravity and weight for the most important person – you!

I always say the Moon landings were faked. Actually I think they went to the Moon. But I am so practiced in the "faked" argument now that I have swung more than one person over to the conspiracy camp.

Practice pleasing yourself - Go your own way daily. At least once a day. Do something that only you will be pleased to do at work or at home. Don't hurt or antagonise of course. But do something that pleases you and not necessarily those around you.

Do Something Unpleasant or Say No Once a Day - Get used to being tough. Make it a point to say no, or do a task you did not want to do every day. White Kangaroo suggests you do this with bills or creditors. I agree.

This builds resilience. If you can respectfully and reasonably say NO to someone even better. This is a habit which you can practice and get better at. It is an important habit to develop for staying within the boundaries of your business plan and in sales/buying negotiations.

6.4. Shaking the Corporate Babble Out of Your Head

Think for Yourself Not the Way HugeCorp tells you - HugeCorp is what the Kangaroo Guides call big business and government establishment. It is time to shake the corporate babble, BS, misdirection and generally useless topics out of your head. You are a Bouncepreneur. You are a real world, small business owner and entrepreneur looking to build a venture to make you rich.

White Kangaroo emphasises that you must start thinking for yourself again.

It is likely that even though you have been an entrepreneur you have in your past:-

- Worked in or for a large organisation
- Been trained in a large organisation
- Adopted key business principles, speech, concepts and beliefs from that business

OR

You have never worked in a big business, but are now digesting all the ideas and direction you can get from the leaders of major enterprises, pearls of wisdom from the CEO of HugeCorp.

<u>Don't listen to HugeCorp!</u>

White Kangaroo always grins as he reminds his students to remember that predictions from HugeCorp analysts and experts have got everything from the Millennium Bug, to the Credit Crunch to the Brexit result wrong.

Wrong, wrong, wrong, wrong, wrong!

So think again, think for yourself and think your own way to success.

Systems - We are told that only big technology systems work. Many voices say big systems are needed before you scale.

White Kangaroo chortles, knowing these voices are selling the software of course.

Simply put if revenue is coming through the door you will quickly resolve your systems problems. Have no doubt of that. Focus on revenue and discoverability first. (More on this later).

Too many experts, institutions and professionals want you to believe that you don't have much choice in the matter. They want to take away your independent thinking because it makes their sales job easier or their profits higher or they have accepted rhetoric of others without thinking for themselves.

You have a lot more choices than you know. You can even skip building the "must do" system altogether.

I once sold a voice technology service that transformed spoken customer responses from surveys to written text. It was great and worked very, very well. But one day I realised it was costing 60 pence to do it through automation and 23 pence to do it with a human being. Plus I was getting more nuance and tone from the human translation AND I was giving local people work they could do at home, between the school run. Plus my own customers wanted suppliers to have a social enterprise element and employing part time Mum's was a big tick in their sourcing box. So I skipped that automation procedure altogether.

Most important on systems is to keep your power to say yes and to say no. Do not follow the pack, choose your own systems.

Tarzan Rope Software Purchasing – imagine Tarzan swinging through the jungle from tree vine to tree vine to get to his beloved Jane. Now imagine that every time he swings from one rope there is another, then another and another. Poor old Tarzan he is spent, exhausted and instead of reaching his goal – seeing Jane he just keeps seeing yet another tree vine that takes real effort to swing from.

Now think of software you have bought. You learn it and then try to make money from it. You need to link it to this other system first, now this plugin, now this bolt-on, now this new channel, now you need images from this tool…. Does it ever stop!

Keep it simple and do not be sucked into spending money and time you haven't got on software that never lets you reach your Jane/Sales!

Business Planning - The stuffed shirts will tell you that you are inadequate if you don't have a 3 year business plan. Well guess what? The 3 year 60 page business plan has past it's sell by date. White Kangaroo simply says "It is the dinosaur of post credit crunch business."

Why? Because technology has obliterated the traditional long term plan. Your product distribution or marketing methods will get turned on its head regularly.

Remember the Mike Tyson golden nugget "Everybody has a plan until they get punched in the face."

The first business plan you will be writing with Bouncepreneurs lasts 30 days and the longest one will last 6 months. (More of that later)

However you DO need to think about two types of business plan – Stuffed Shirt and Real.

The Stuffed Shirt one you need for your bank, or other body who request it and are a gate keeper to a service or market you need.

Your Real Business Plan. Good business planning is desperately needed - but it should be planning on **your** terms. Good planning has several key elements and White Kangaroo encourages you to:-

- It is written by you and for you AND no-one else – no approval needed
- It uses language, terms and financials you understand fully
- It expects change
- You look at it daily
- And you WANT to look at it daily
- It is scribbled on, coffee stained, tattered from over use.
- Your financial spreadsheets are the most used file on your computer

Dismiss is the old formal 3, 5, 10 year business plan document. Not planning itself.

Sales and Marketing - You have to sell online – to sell online you have to have discoverability. You have to, otherwise no-one sees your products.

But online is NOT the only channel open to you. It isn't!

But White Kangaroo asks you to break "online" down for a moment.

You can have a lovely web presence. Great little website, with a nice form for enquiries and maybe a lovely e-commerce and fulfilment set up.

But you do not HAVE to use paid social media to drive customers there. And maybe you cannot afford it in the beginning anyway.

So your online presence can be more about making it easy for people to UNDERSTAND YOUR OFFER and to REFER their friends to you. But maybe not the place where they initially find you.

If they can find you too. Then happy days. But this maybe a two stage process.

But as White Kangaroo emphasises DISCOVERABILITY is critical.

You have to be discoverable for customers to find you on Facebook, Twitter, LinkedIn, Pinterest even if you don't have money for paid advertising.

Online Marketing Can Dominate Your Business to Point of Failure – Organic SEO growth, even using SEO systems like Yoast is hard, hard work.

So many Bouncepreneurs who have made it back, talk about how their failed business required them to work for hour after hour learning new software and there was never an end in sight.

Today's online sales and marketing is like a Russian Doll in reverse. You start with a small simple piece of software. You do your work and then press the activate button online to find you need to plugin to another piece of software (a larger Russian Doll) which involves some cost and is a little more complicated. You work on this and what do you know, it leads you to yet another Doll/application you need to work on to reach your sales and marketing goal. And on and on.

Then at the end you find you have a huge Russian Doll, with no customers and six months gone by. Worse still you have no online discoverability, no one knows you. Or worse the prospects you have got are poor in the extreme. And you have no money left to pay for the advertising needed to gain visibility.

You Have to Do Everything Online - You don't have to. Online should achieve these things for a start-up:-

- Bring you customers
- Be manageable
- Lower costs
- Make you more efficient
- Your online tasks can be delegated once you have shaken them down

If your online activities don't do this – then just don't do them.

Word of Mouth Doesn't Work Anymore -Word of mouth certainly does work. But it has evolved into viral marketing.

Word of mouth is great. Jack tells Sam about your product Sam buys. But you really need Jack to tell all his friends on social media and your materials are so good it spreads.

So essentially you want customers to talk about your service to each other without being prompted. You cannot force an idea to go viral. But if you can get an "ideavirus" going you don't need to do anymore marketing. The population will spread the word by themselves.

The Chinese make Everything Cheaper - There is a culture in the UK and in other countries which suggests we cannot compete with cheap imports from China and similar low cost economies.

If you have a manufacturing idea in mind for your next business then go for it. If anybody says you won't compete with the Chinese I have one word for you to say to them.

"Germany"

This view is propagated by a generation of politicos and consultants who know little outside of financial services and outsourcing.

Don't accept it. If you think you can manufacture then do it. Just make sure it is profitable and you can somehow manage the capital equipment costs.

UK entrepreneurs are already showing this fear of all things manufacturing by reinvigorating industries on smaller scale than in the past, but owner-manged shoe making is a good example.

Remember it takes 28 days to ship from China and like other countries quality is there to be bettered.

Export - Export is difficult for start-ups is another myth. Sure it is administration. But that is work. Work is what you do says the White Kangaroo.

To be a successful exporter you need four main things:-

- Demand
- Profitability
- Solid local distribution
- Competence with administration

Sure markets change, administration burdens change and distribution partnership change. But it should not stop you.

Bear in mind the Chinese don't like eating locally produced food because of the pollution in their atmosphere. It is a great export opportunity, simple as that.

Not everything is price driven either is it Bouncepreneur? But you already know that.

CEO Heroes - You must emulate the great leaders and CEO's of big businesses. I don't think this is quite right. If you can deconstruct and see how they got the business off the ground from Day 1 then fabulous. These people deserve your respect.

But corporate leaders ARE not start up entrepreneurs and often not Bouncepreneurs.

Well you must emulate their first few years if they founded the business for sure. But if they joined the business when it "only had" 60 stores (like Howard Schulz of Starbucks did) it is hardly a small business is it! 60 stores. 60 stores! Sorry Howard I love my Pike's Place coffee and especially the fact that you offer it at an affordable price plus refills for those on a budget. The team in my local Wrexham Starbucks are a delight.

White Kangaroo tells us we may have huge admiration for many big business leaders. But to hold them up to start up entrepreneurs to follow is often not right. Blind hero worship of CEO's who have taken on major business with huge start-up capital does not reflect the reality of entrepreneurship when you are starting with nothing, your own savings or a small bank loan.

As White Kangaroo says – Apples and Pears.

So be careful who you follow. If your hero has not felt the pain of being really broke, having to rebuild with worn out tools or failed, then they should be respected of course, but they are not in the Bouncepreneur tribe.

White Kangaroo strongly recommends you read business autobiographies. Libraries stock them and they are free to borrow you know. Fancy that free books you can borrow. Fancy that! Now that's a modern disruptive business model isn't it?

Make your CEO heroes those who have started the business from scratch, like Lika Shing of Cheung Kong Industries. Mr Shing is an amazing man. Mr Shing even lost part of a finger working in a company where he learnt the plastics business and went on to found his own company.

I saw a business growth programme which used Cirque de Soleil as an illustration for an entrepreneurial success. But what is didn't say was the founder Laliberte flew his troupe from Canada in the early days to perform in Los Angeles with no money to fly them back! I don't suppose he was too bothered with a 3 year business plan when the fire breather was asking the times of the return flights.

Team- You need a great team around you. Is that true. Yes for sure. But do you need to follow the same path as HugeCorp.

White Kangaroo tells his student to avoid emulating HugeCorp on people motivation. Pay your people and give them the excitement and opportunity that only a rapidly growing business can offer. Leave the chill out room for HugeCorp.

You need competent reliable, people to implement your plan. You don't always need innovation. If your team have a great idea then use it. But you don't need people to challenge your strategy. Tactics yes, but strategy no. You are the Leader. You!

Concentrate on preparing very clear job roles and action plans. Very, very clear. By having done the job role yourself before you hand it over to an employee you will have a better understanding of what your employee may be capable of delivering. But you will be handing over to your Kangaroo Sergeant-Majors. They WILL follow your strategy?

I was once in an interview with a prospective employee who said to me very directly "Michael I am a single mother, I need a stable job 9-5. I don't need pressure to work late as I want to be with my daughter. I will give you 100% while I am here, but please don't judge me on my willingness to stay late as you are not going to get me outside of 9-5."

She was one of my best employees and changed my thinking on great employees. Get people who can deliver your plan. Keep your plan simple.

Remember, you are the leader. It is your business, your risk and your wealth.

By having clear simple roles you can get your business up to a good size.

Don't employ people to break new ideas ground for you. Do that yourself. By handling off each major area of the business to staff in turn as you work it out and simplify it. Once all your key roles are handed off, then you get the time you then get to yourself you can use to plan innovation and business evolution.

You are not KPMG, Unilever, Dell, 3M or BMW. So don't try to play like them. Keep the business beautifully simple. Employ key people in a limited number of uncomplicated roles.

Think of replacing yourself in one on the following areas at a time.

- Sales & Marketing
- The Factory – where you make or do
- Finance & Admin
- Customer Service

That's it!

You Need MBA's in Your Business – Maybe you don't need MBA's. Maybe they are a liability to focus. Maybe they will try to change your plan and not follow it. Also they are going to expect to be paid more. HugeCorp can have them.

If you hold an MBA, put your business skills to the test and go for it. Good luck.

You need an organisation chart in your start up plan – No you don't you need to have job descriptions, based on the first four people you wat to employ. But only do that when you have the absolute certainty you know what you need to tell them to do.

Consultants - Consultants earn big money – you do not need them – even the free ones.

But if you go to LinkedIn you see loads of them wandering around looking for work, crumbs from HugeCorp's table. Trying to show they have the latest knowledge and tell everyone else they need to change. Then they are pitching to executives whose own tenure in HugeCorp is far from safe.

The model is broken. The big Enterprises are slashing costs through offshoring, technology shift and mergers. Working for HugeCorp as a consultant is a guarantee of uncertainty of income. Don't you think about that type of business. You can do something far better!

Tendering - Tendering is fair. If you have poor credit ratings OR you have lost a business through bankruptcy or liquidation you have little chance of getting work through tendering. With buying consortiums becoming more common and sharing knowledge more frequently, getting work as a failed entrepreneur can be very, very difficult indeed. So be realistic about this. Do not sucked into time-consuming wasted effort.

Outsourcing Customer Service - HugeCorp is driving down customer service costs across the global economy. This presents some huge opportunities for Bouncepreneurs and start-ups generally. But not as a supplier to HugeCorp – no. Rather to fill the gaps that HugeCorp leave behind.

The HugeCorp agenda has been:-

Shut retail in your town > Go to call centre > Outsource call centre >

Offshore call centre > Switch voice service to online or app or IVR > Kill off voice service

Now this provides two great opportunities for entrepreneurs

a. You can provide a personalised service to smaller numbers of customers (but still massive numbers to a small business) who want and are prepared to pay for higher quality service support

b. The technologies developed by HugeCorp and its major suppliers have been copied and made cheaper allowing you to deliver the same type of low cost service. So if you have a better product you have a competitive advantage.

Profitability Corporate Margins versus Entrepreneur Margins – "you cannot compete with the big boys because of their margins." White Kangaroo chuckles at this. The pressures on executives to deliver growth in profitability to the shareholders is huge. But you do not need to compare your profits to theirs. If you were trying to go toe to toe with a car manufacturer you might get slaughtered because you cannot afford the same investment to build comparable products. But if you have a popular product people want to buy and you have fans who love your product, then your relative profitability to HugeCorp is irrelevant.

So long as you have profit that is making YOU rich and your business is growing through scalability, repeatability and you are not working 24/7 on the operation then ignore your margins relative to the big boys.

3rd Party Market Research is Worthwhile - As a big part of my career has been involved in market and customer research I give the following advice for start-ups. DON'T rely on research reports.

Get out and do you own research. Also don't rely on a questionnaire. YOU MUST dig deeper. The best way to really test your idea is to actually ask people to buy it. NOT "if I make it will you buy it," but "I have some ready now (even if you don't) do you want to buy them? They cost £/$/€ each."

The reaction to this question is the key. Build a one page website with details of your offering, a simple sales deck too. Try and sell and check the reaction. This is the critical path and far more worthwhile than 3rd party research. More on this with Green Kangaroo later.

White Kangaroo always tells his students to beware of many research reports on overseas markets are written by analysts who haven't even been there. They are just recycling other online material. If you are exporting get out there and see for yourself.

FMCG is the Domain of Big Business – you may have read that just a handful of massive Hugecorps are now dominating the global food industry. All I know is all the chocolate I grew up on now tastes like wax and the bars are half the size. So I save myself up for a chocolate fest with the good stuff on my travels.

So in food, why do we need to eat plastic bread, crackers with chocolate and drinks packed with sugar? Why do we put that crap in our bodies? Why!

So there is plenty of opportunity to make and sell food and other FMCG items of higher quality, nutrition and social value.

Automation is Essential – no it isn't. If you can find other ways to avoid capital equipment costs in your early days, then go for it. Your main goal is to scale, repeat and get out within a year of the operation and achieve profit. It is not to tie yourself into long term investment into equipment.

Customers are now your Competitors – White Kangaroo has another warning to all the consultants our there chasing contracts with HugeCorp. The guy or girl you are sitting opposite, working for HugeCorp does not have stable employment. They really don't. In leadership roles in customer service for example the average length of a manager's employment is 2-4 years. Then they join the LinkedIn herd of wanderers trying to get crumbs from HugeCorp's table.

So if you go in with a service idea, or a consulting proposition you could easily be giving it to a competitor and not a potential customer. Another reason why one man consultancy is for mugs.

Foreign Money Spends the Same – As an entrepreneur you can take your business into new markets. One Bouncepreneur I met was fed up of failing to win tenders for his small road-building company. The contracts he did get to keep him going drove him to the verge of personal bankruptcy. When he reset his new business he explored and won road building work in countries in Africa and remote former Soviet states. The business flourished. He said to me "Once you get a £ pound from a client in Botswana you can spend it the same as a £ pound from England."

White Kangaroo's Key Lessons

White Kangaroo has given you a number of ways to blanch and acid-strip your mind of redundant ideas which do not serve you well.

He has encouraged you to begin thinking unconventionally. You have read his irreverent challenge to HugeCorp and those lazy advisory ideas which bog your thinking down.

White Kangaroo is pleased to have given you fresh thinking towards business in terms of fighting for your prosperity and happiness.

He wishes you good fortune and now hands you over to his colleague Yellow Kangaroo. She is going to show you how to generate bright Ideas for you new venture.

CONGRATULATIONS YOU ARE NOW A WHITE BELT BOUNCEPRENEUR!

7 Yellow Kangaroo Generating Bright Ideas

7.1. Introduction

Yellow Kangaroo is such a bright personality. She is as yellow as sunshine with a personality and clothes to match. Where did she find that hat? Some say she drinks a little too much caffeine for her own good. But there is no doubting her energy in supporting idea generation.

Yellow Kangaroo is here to help you take the best business ideas forward into further testing and live launch.

You will find her a great guide for the creative process of coming up with ideas. But you will also see like all her fellow Kangaroo Guides she has a tough side too. Yellow Kangaroo will never criticise an idea or put down your creativity NEVER. She hates that in fact. With a vengeance.

But she will harass you constantly to ensure you are not emotionally over-attached to any one business idea OR you are deliberately kidding yourself about the viability of your idea.

Ultimately the decision on which business idea you take forward is down to you. BUT make sure you are objective and professional says Yellow Kangaroo.

7.2. Product or Service Selection, test and Launch

Yellow Kangaroo often shocks her new Bouncepreneurs by saying from the outset

"Your new business launch and your business model testing are one and the same thing."

That's right. You are going to launch a product with the following objectives

1st Earn

2nd Learn

If you do not earn then you have learnt enough about your product idea.

Trust Yellow Kangaroo this is the best way to succeed and will reduce risk of failure and wasted investment (which is tough to get in the first place right).

7.3. Pet Projects

Now before you get going a few house rules for you budding Bouncepreneurs.

Please, Please, Please begs Yellow Kangaroo - do NOT have a pet idea and keep it intact despite clear evidence it may not be a good idea. Don't pay lip service towards the process. Generate multiple ideas so that you have a fall back to bring forward in case your pet project shows itself flawed.

Same goes for restarting your previous business (Life Boat Business), by all means put it in as an idea during brain storming, but treat it the same as any other different ideas you have.

This business is not the love of your life. You can be passionate about what you are doing to help customers, but be objective about this project. Think like a Professional Entrepreneur.

Think that this business will have a life span of 2-5 years. It may go on past that point, with or without you. Thinking in these terms sharpens your approach to this business concept as a money making enterprise.

7.4. Yellow Kangaroo's Guide to Brainstorming

You may already have a business idea in your mind. Maybe you don't. Or you may have more than one. We recommend you develop multiple ideas throughout your brainstorming at this point.

Read and follow Yellow Kangaroo's Guides below. She gives you plenty of ideas on a brainstorming methods you can try.

OBJECTIVE – At the end of your brainstorming work have a list of all the ideas you feel have merit. You may have 2 to 5 ideas. Don't go forward with just one. It may cause too narrow a thinking process for you.

Then run them through the screening process further on. You should be left with one strongest idea and maybe a couple of backups.

To be clear, you may have to do most of this brain storming on your own. But if you have three or four trusted friends or family make a huge pan of spaghetti and bring them round to throw around ideas. You can do this more than once, maybe you can ask three or four business people you know and respect for a coffee together in Starbucks to toss around concepts. It all helps. Remember says Yellow Kangaroo, these are only ideas so you can be a little wild at this point.

Why? Because your main idea may fall over in the testing process and we want the idea you go forward with the best idea to give you the maximum chance of success.

You may just come up with an idea you develop later on, when you have deeper pockets. So save those for the future. Remember Bouncepreneurs have multiple businesses in time! You can start with a very modest project.

Yellow Kangaroo's Pre-Brainstorming Ground Rules

Some of you have brainstormed before. Yellow Kangaroo says we all need some brainstorming ground rules.

Firstly we are trying to generate ideas for a new business to make you Rich and Happy.

You just need to FIRST generate a list of ideas and we MUST NOT judge them during idea generation at this stage.

Because you may be working solo, then get a little notebook or note taking app and try to write down at least three ideas a day for a week. This should get you going.

Remember - it won't be your only business. You will have others. You are building Money Engines. So if you have a second or third great idea, then save it, as you may be returning to it.

You may come up with ideas that you don't like very much, but keep them in the process. Remember "where's there's muck there is brass." There is money in the work no-one else fancies doing.

Yellow Kangaroo's Recommended Brainstorming Methods

Here are some great methods for brainstorming – some new, some old. Pick one you like best and generate some business ideas. All you need is a big pad of paper! Go Go Go Bouncepreneur! Tells Yellow Kangaroo in her normal energy packed way.

<u>Brainstorming around a Problem or Opportunity</u> – this is a bit different because you start brainstorming business ideas based around a specific problem. For example swimming pools are not used late at night, but have to be heated when empty. Or children are not exercising enough, or most takeaways throw their vegetable oil cans into the rubbish bin. Focus on a problem that you have noticed and brainstorm business ideas around solving the problem or seizing on the opportunity.

<u>A to B</u> this is Yellow Kangaroo's favourite method. You start with the customer you would like to help, who you know has a problem. For example, helping families on limited budgets improve their kid's diets. A is poor diet, B is great diet – you just come up with as many crazy ideas as you can. Don't worry about the crazy ones. It all helps.

<u>Quentin Tarantino Brainstorming</u> - Think about blending ideas together – that's how Quentin Tarantino comes up with his film concepts apparently. He himself described "Pulp Fiction" as a rock 'n' roll spaghetti western with surf music and "Django" as a western proper with a southern slavery backdrop. If food is a business you want to get into think flavours. Black current and liquorice ice cream – the work of genius and Yellow Kangaroo's favourite, mine too!

<u>Changing Who You Are</u> - You can think of yourself as a completely different person OR change one or two things about yourself. A good one here is age – younger or older. With an aging population services and products for the aged are going to grow for sure. But you can think about a different gender, your race, religion, fitness or weight. These different perspectives will make a difference in how you see things and this will help ideas flow. Every time you change a feature, you will see things very differently and again ideas will flow.

<u>Ten Minute Writing Frenzy</u> – This is a great method if you are on your own. You set an alarm for exactly ten minutes. Then you start, forcing yourself to write down every idea or concept or thought that pops into your head. No judgement, no review, just pure ideas. Even those of you who simply do not know what to put down on paper, eventually have a breakthrough and when that dam bursts ideas keep on flowing. You are switching on the sub-conscious element of your mind and there is gold in there, promises Yellow Kangaroo.

<u>Group Brainstorming</u> – if you want to try a group brainstorm it is better to get someone to run it for you. You can act as an observer. Try to stay focused on key ideas at first. Don't scrutinise them until later. When you start discussing ideas as a group, you will get lots of wide and various ideas. Always good to include younger adults as they tend to be more creative.

One key tip – if you get one person dominating discussion, on or before the halfway point ask them (nicely) to leave. This will allow you to hear the ideas of others as well.

<u>Using an Asset</u> - Maybe you have an asset, an orchard, some land, a garage a huge pile of wood, a large group of friends, maybe even a language or in depth knowledge of a foreign country. Consider every crazy idea you can think of to make this asset sweat for you. Don't let anything be out of bounds when you brainstorm.

<u>Future Trends</u> – brainstorm around a topic of change you know is going to be happening in the future. Think about opportunities this might present, it might be political change or aging populations. Maybe you think that voice technology is going to be huge, maybe Brexit will lead to big changes in the fishing industry, and perhaps you think sugar is going to be banned. Start with a key trend you feel attracted to. Start with a concept such as – after Brexit the UK may have sole (not lemon sole) rights to fishing in its territorial waters. What opportunities might this create in the UK or on the European Continent? Just keep writing down ideas.

<u>Role playing or Cosplay Even</u> – in this method you assume the persona of someone you really admire. For me I really admire Andrew Probert one of the founders of the hugely successful Admiral Insurance, whom I had the pleasure of going on a long road trip with years ago. Andrew was all about remaining cost competitive and running a leaner ship than the competition. So my own role play is thinking that I am Andrew and creating ideas as he might. I might even put on a pullover that I remember him wearing which was covered in diamond shapes. You might like to indulge in a little Cosplay too. So if you are thinking like Richard Branson stick on a false beard. Anything to get the ideas flowing. Remember think not as yourself but as Andrew or Richard. Put yourself in their mind set.

<u>Doctor Who Time Traveller</u> – imagine you are Doctor Who and have landed the Tardis in the future. Think about the sector or industry you think there might be an opportunity. With all the future technology at your disposal how might you tackle this problem and give customers something they would really want. Brainstorm from a future perspective and ideas will start to generate.

<u>Mind Mapping</u> is a highly proven brainstorming. It is simply you writing your broadest concept (for example nutrition, publishing or cars) in the centre of a big sheet of paper or board, then breaking it down into subcategory ideas. Create as many subcategories as you can plus any ideas that jump out as you go.

<u>Superpower</u> You get any super power you want. Except the super power of absorbing all other super powers because apparently my daughter took that one first! But think if you had ANY superpower, how would that change your brainstorming session? Maybe you can freeze things on a whim, lift cars with one hand, change your appearance to any other person or even fly. Try as many superpowers as possible to see things from lots of angles. It sounds crazy, but it can lead to some great ideas this one.

<u>Copy Others</u> – think about a really effective idea (that made someone rich and happy) and take it to another market or place. I once saw a fantastic ice cream parlour on a trip to the Netherlands. It was fabulous with both adults and children alike loving to go there. I will one day try to recreate this concept elsewhere. If I don't eat all the ice cream first. Brainstorm things you have seen working elsewhere and see what you come up with

<u>Nearly Worked</u> – think about businesses you have seen fail, businesses that have not quite made it and owners have left behind. Throw these ideas into your pot too. There might be a way of taking them forward successfully. Sometimes it is all about timing.

7.5. Your Best Idea

Write Down Your Best Ideas Here. Give them all equal billing at this point. Yellow Kangaroo has a reminder for you - Try not to let your heart pull you towards a favourite.

Best Ideas for My New Venture List	
Idea Name	Idea Description

7.6. Screening Your Ideas Guidelines and Considerations

When screening your ideas, please be professional and honest with yourself. Please follow Yellow Kangaroos Ten Commandments of Business Idea Screening.

Yellow Kangaroos Ten Commandments of Business Idea Screening

1. Do not have a pet idea you are going to keep come what may
2. Do not be precious about working in a familiar business environment or sector
3. Be prepared to dump a bad idea
4. Be prepared to change direction on your idea (swivel)
5. Be prepared to spot a parallel idea which is better than yours during the testing process
6. Be very honest with yourself
7. Absolutely promise not to have an irrational attachment to a bad idea or previous business model that failed.
8. Remember all business is easy when you have income coming in
9. Don't abuse customer time or trust during the testing process
10. Don't rely on the opinion of friends (test your ideas with strangers)

One of the great benefits of going with the **Scale Up - Duplicate – Get Out (SUDGO)** method is the way it can quickly clean out bad ideas.

In other idea testing models one tends to look only at the customer problem, competition and customer value. Now these are important. But there is no point in getting these three things right if the business is not scalable, or you cannot duplicate it, or get out of operating it to leave it to trusted lieutenants.

Now if you have fast tracked your pet idea through to this stage, take special note. You must test it with the same vigour as any other ideas.

Be a Professional Entrepreneur now and not a Broke Entrepreneur in 6 months. Now is the time to be diligent.

Before you screen your ideas, here are a few final considerations for you to make.

Yellow Kangaroo's Business Idea Selection - Considerations

Make sure you **pick a business idea that customers actually want!** Yellow Kangaroo smiles as she reminds us that entrepreneurs launch ideas that nobody wants every day. Thousands have done it and will do it. She encourages you to find a great idea people want. She wants you to become rich and happy.

Her best advice is to go for a business idea that will shine by addressing <u>one</u> small problem really well. Really, really well.

Do not forget to **site your business in the right place** – I was once involved with picking store locations in UK cities. Our brief was to pick cheap sites. So the sites we picked were low cost on industrial estates off the beaten track. The competitor who had exactly the same model picked prime sites with lots of passing trade in cars. Our chain lasted less than a year, the competitor was Halfords a huge success.

Choose an idea that doesn't have to educate people – as a Bouncepreneur with limited funds Yellow Kangaroo warns us that we cannot afford to educate your market into liking your product or changing deeply ingrained habits. You may be totally justified in believing you have a better solution for your customer than competitors. But unless they get it straightaway you will wither and die financially trying to show them "the light."

Don't call the customer's baby ugly is also a good idea. This mistake is very common in markets where the customer is already part of a tribe. If they are part of a trade body in a B2B industry, chances are they use the association's quality standard, their training courses, go to their awards, and may have won a trophy. Their trade friends and network are also involved. If you go in there with a rival product, chances are they will hate you for it, just like a pack of wolves hates a wolf from another pack. Best avoided.

Yellow Kangaroo has seen too many Bouncepreneurs biting off more than they can chew. Like all Kangaroos she really knows a thing or two about chewing. Chose a business idea that you are able to pull off – **don't you bite off more than you can chew**. Think about a business that will gain traction and revenue without you having to buy a ship, or a fleet of planes or a £100 million digital printer. You do not have to create your perfect product right away, one that gets revenue flowing and customer's happy is good enough. As you build more and more businesses you can afford bigger and bigger start-up costs.

Be happy says Yellow Kangaroo, but don't fall in love. Go for compatibility with your values rather than the love of your life. Yellow Kangaroo insists if you are making enough money then you will learn to love ANY industry again! Choose a business idea you want to run - Some of us have spent many years working in an industry we don't like anymore. I know I have seen enough call centres for a long time. But I worked in food packaging years ago and loved it. Seeing Mars Bars, Vienetta Ice Cream, Cadbury Cream Eggs and Coca Cola drinks made was great fun. I loved it. So jump into an idea in an industry you're enthusiastic about. But do remember you are going to get out of operations within a year. So it does not have to be a life time love affair.

Try to choose a business idea that really stands out – for your entrepreneurial idea to make you rich it <u>has</u> to stand out. Be bold advises Yellow Kangaroo. It doesn't have to be entirely new. It may just be beautifully done. Me and Yellow Kangaroo once went to a wedding together in Poland (what can I say I am a cheap date) we were amazed by huge glass vases full of stunning flowers submerged in water. At night they were backlit with coloured lights and were amazing. I had never seen anything like it in the UK. It was the same flowers I might see at a UK wedding but sunk it water and lit up at night. Remember customer problems (creating a stunning wedding reception in this case) will bring in lots of competition. So make sure your idea really does stand out.

Yellow Kangaroo reminds you of another concept. Why not **transfer ideas from one market to another** – karaoke is a classic example. Most homes in the West have a device or app that has evolved from the Japanese love of singing. If you are able to find an idea hidden away in a market far far from your own, import it. This also counts for B2B and industrial products.

One more time Yellow Kangaroo advises caution if you are **choosing a business idea because you have done it before** - if you have tried this idea and failed, then you really need to ask yourself why it will work this time around. In the next chapter we will scrutinise business ideas very, very thoroughly and hopefully any lasting emotional attachment for a lost business/bad idea will be finally "put to the sword".

Don't choose a business idea that customers can't/won't pay for – Make sure you control access to your product. If customers want it, they need to pay for it. I have done this myself. I built a fantastic benchmarking tool for B2B customers. It was light years ahead of the competition. But when I took it to market I was amazed to see wholesale distribution of the login details amongst major firms to avoid paying the subscription. I had not expected FTSE500 and government agencies to follow this route – but they did! I failed to secure access properly and didn't realise that although nearly everyone in the industry wanted it, most had no budgetary authority to buy it and others would resort to getting an illegal copy for free. It was a tough lesson indeed.

7.7. Now Screen Your Shortlisted Ideas

Below we have a screening audit for your business ideas. Run each of your ideas through the audit in turn. Take the total score and place it in the Best Ideas Comparison Table below.

Here are some questioning thoughts to help you fill in this table.

- Does your customer have money to buy your product or service?
- Are they prepared to pay enough to make it worthwhile?
- Do you feel you have the time and money to start this business?
- Does your business idea fit in with where you currently live?
- Do you have the skills/expertise to deliver a very basic version of this product to customers as a trial?
- Do you think the profit margin will be healthy?
- Does your product have a repeat buy element?
- Can you product be sold as a club with a subscription?
- Can you sell this product off plan, without building any?

#	Factor	Question to Be Answered	Your rating/answers	Score
		Bouncepreneurs Venture Idea Screening Process (Score 5 = very good 1= very bad)		
1	Customer Problem	Have you clearly identified a customer problem that is not being adequately addressed? What is this problem	Write down the problem and rate you own confidence in the fact it is not being addressed adequately	
2	Competition	Is the level of competition going to be a hindrance to your ability to scale up your business?	Think about where you are going to trade. If you are in a small town with 70 hairdressers then you are not going to gain a bridgehead to springboard scale from are you? Write down the impact of competition on your ability to scale up and duplicate the idea	
3	Customer Value	Do you think the customer will perceive value and buy it? (more on this later)	Write down why and rate your level of confidence on this fact.	
4	Scale Up	Can you scale revenue up nationally or internationally?	Describe you first second and third sites or market places	

5	Duplicate	Can you duplicate the process many times?	What impact on your operating costs will increased sales have? Write down what you think	
6	Getoutable	Can the work be done without you?	Can the business run without you? Can you entirely delegate key modules within your business? Write down why you think this and how you would delegate	
7	Risk	Biggest Risk of this idea. Write it down here	Write down what key risk must be satisfied in order for the venture to succeed.	
	TOTAL SCORE			

Now in the Best Ideas Comparison Table put in your key ideas with their score. Any niggles or considerations that are on your mind, put them down too.

Best Ideas Comparison Table			
Idea Name	Niggles or Considerations	Score	Rank
			1st
			2nd
			3rd
			4th
			5th

7.8. Yellow Kangaroo's Key Lessons

In this Chapter Yellow Kangaroo has given us a solid start to developing and screening our new venture ideas.

But she herself admits this level of idea testing is not strong enough for great Bouncepreneurs. Yellow Kangaroo has helped you get your idea juices flowing - well done, great job.

She is sad to see you go, but you are always welcome to revisit her in future and there is no shame in coming back. None at all. Better to start again and get the right idea than fail again on the wrong one.

Now Yellow Kangaroo is going to pass you over to your next Guide – Orange Kangaroo. Orange Kangaroo is a purely logical thinker. Some say he is the Spock of the Kangaroo Guides, you might agree. I do. Orange does not have any sentimentality or emotion in his whole body.

CONGRATULATIONS YOU ARE NOW A YELLOW BELT BOUNCEPRENEUR

8 Orange Kangaroo and the 7 Orange Fences

8.1. Introduction

If you look at Orange Kangaroo you will see his ears are a little pointier than his fellow Bouncepreneur Guides. It is the Vulcan in him. He really is a serious, no nonsense fellow. Orange Kangaroo takes his job very, very seriously.

His main message to his Bouncepreneur students is "Measure Twice Cut Once!" He uses this old tailoring phrase over and over again.

He really encourages you to LET GO OF BEING RIGHT and to be prepared to accept that your best venture idea might not be viable.

Orange Kangaroo really tried to ensure that you go forward with a business venture idea that really is going to work. But even then when you meet the next Guide - Green Kangaroo your idea testing will not be over by the way.

Orange Kangaroo's main job is to ensure you launch a successful venture.

You know it is not just the money you waste investing, when you go to market with a flawed idea, it is the time. Plus there is the time you have wasted earning nothing when you could have been earning big money too.

The selection of your next venture matters, the impacts of your decision are very, very real indeed.

I am speaking by the way as someone who HAS picked some really poor ideas.

I wasted at least a year on most of them too!

A year! A whole year

AND I have done that 4 times!

So I have wasted four years of my life and many thousands of pounds on ideas that could have been more thoroughly tested and swivelled to a better idea or simply culled.

And I was a PROFESSIONAL MARKET RESEARCHER!

Please learn from me. If not yourself.

So if you are reading this now with a single idea in your head (especially the relaunch of your old failed business) then you MUST be prepared to see it rejected.

<u>You cannot take it personally.</u>

When the test process rejects your idea, or it is significantly modified, you have learned a valuable lesson about your strategy. The fact your idea did not fly is not a reflection on your worth as a business person or human.

Orange Kangaroo will support you fully if you are BIG ENOUGH to abandon or change an idea you are personally invested in. This makes you a professional entrepreneur, more than anything else.

8.2. Getting your Product Right is More Important than You Being Right

In the next Chapter, Orange Kangaroo will help you take your idea testing further.

Be prepared to maybe find your idea rejected. You may even be stunned that guinea pig customers will reject or struggle with your idea – an idea that made so much sense to you!

Orange Kangaroo himself does not feel emotion, so he is not fazed by getting ideas wrong. He simply goes on to the next one for testing. This is where being a professional entrepreneur comes in. So many times Amateur Entrepreneurs (and HugeCorp) have a knee-jerk reaction to unfavourable, poor customer feedback. They simply resort to being and thinking negatively about the trial users that they are:-

- Plain wrong and others will get it
- They are not that clever and not actually the target customer after all
- They forget the customer has choice – a choice of which service/product to use and a choice to go elsewhere

Now, Orange Kangaroo tells us a Professional Entrepreneur thinks differently and knows

- The user's problem is the Professional Entrepreneur's problem, and to be a successful the product/service has to be met the problem, modified or even scrapped
- They recognise the product's flaws if the customer finds it too complicated to figure out service.
- They are acutely aware the customer can go without this solution
- Or they can go to a competitor
- They know the customer does not care that the Entrepreneur worked really hard on this idea
- Finally, they know the customer only cares whether or not your solution solves their problem

Professional Entrepreneurs think of prototypes and hypothesises, advises Orange Kangaroo. He emphasises that your first attempt might not quite work and that is okay. Because your goal is to learn what works and what does not, swivel, make improvements, and test again.

It is quite likely you may end up with a product that is very different from the one you originally planned. But becoming RICH and HAPPY is all about being able to detach yourself emotionally from your product, allowing a cool, cold Professional Entrepreneur's mind to make informed decisions.

8.3. Rely on What Customer's Do and not what they Say they do

It is worth noting Bouncepreneur (advices Orange Kangaroo) that market research techniques and ideas testing has been going through something of a "tug of war" in very recent times. This is very relevant to you AND to the method we are going to suggest you use.

There is the traditional product testing method encouraging you to

- Interview potential users
- Do online research on competitors and customers
- Running focus groups

This concept is to let the customer guide you. Orange Kangaroo sees merit in this and no reason why you should not use these techniques to better inform your choice of business venture. But be very, very, VERY careful.

Henry Ford is often quoted as saying "If I had asked people what they wanted, they would have said faster horses."

There is a school of thought that says you should not rely on what the customer tells you they will do or buy in the market research phased. Orange Kangaroo is a big fan of this thinking and suggests you should be too. I qualified in market research 3 decades before writing this book and I agree with the Orange Guide too.

According to Eric Ries Author of a great book The Lean Startup

"Customers don't know what they want. There is plenty of good psychology research that shows that people are not accurately able to predict how they would behave in the future. So asking them "would you buy my product if it had these three features?" or "How would you react if we changed our product in this way?" is a waste of time. They don't know."

Because someone tells you they would use your service or product, does not guarantee they really will. People are terribly flawed at predicting their future behaviour. That is why when you are testing your product ideas you can only put so much reliance onto your research findings – no matter how diligently you did the survey or focus group work.

8.4. Minimum Viable Product/Money Where Your Mouth Is

The idea of the Minimum Viable Product has emerged as an alternative to traditional market research methods for testing out not product and service ideas. It is a very good approach – especially for cash-strapped Bouncepreneurs.

It is effect the entrepreneur taking the most basic version of her product to market and saying to customers

"There it is- buy it and buy it now" as a means of testing demand.

Orange Kangaroo strongly advises you that this really is the best way to test if your product or service idea is going to make you rich.

We are going to take a very close look at this in the next Chapter. But be aware that this type of investigation requires an ACTUAL product launch. So Orange Kangaroo emphasises the need for close attention to his methods in the remainder of this Chapter.

After all you do not want to go to the trouble of launching a venture idea you have not thoroughly tested – do you?

That type of thinking is for Amateur Entrepreneurs and you are not one of them are you?

The Bouncepreneur MVP method is different from the standard MVP process. Why? Because it builds into the testing process checks on ensuring your business idea can be Scaled Up – Duplicated – Getoutable (SUDGO).

DO NOT go to market flat out based purely on market research. It is just too risky.

Most importantly of all do not ask what people want. Instead, find out what they need.

Establish what problems already exist. Play with understanding how people _deal_ with these problems. Be obsessive about this. Keep asking the same questions over and over.

Do not be thinking about your solution at all at this stage. That comes later. Right now you must be the "fly on the wall" watch behaviour, identify pain points THEN determine what needs to be built.

8.5. The 7 Fence Challenge to a Solid Product/Service Testing Process

Orange Kangaroo says if you can clear all 7 Fences then you have a good business idea.

Kangaroos like your Orange Guide are resourceful animals. They are real entrepreneurs always looking for an opportunity to roam happily and to eat rich food.

But they face a problem. Fences.

All over the place fences.

The fences are a metaphor for testing a good business idea. This will test your business idea in your own mind before you spend serious time, money and effort bringing it to market.

You can clear a fence this means that specific element of your idea is solid.

If you can see no way over or around a fence, this means your idea is fatally flawed and you need to go back to your next business idea. The idea is flawed if you are not able to clear any 1 fence. Orange Kangaroo reminds you that you have to clear ALL 7 to have a solid business idea.

Or you cannot clear a fence with your idea as it stands, but if you change an element of your idea then it may work. Imagine Orange Kangaroo up against a fence he cannot jump. He needs a Swivel Point left or right until he finds another approach to clearing the fence.

This Swivel Point will allow you to keep the core of the idea. But you MUST change this element and not simply launch it. This change might be, for example, to address a new target group. It might mean a change to a feature of your product to better meet the needs of your customer OR any of the underlying 7 Fence tests which are

The 7 Fence Tests

1. Who is the customer who has the money to spend?
2. How many like them are there?
3. What issue are you solving for this customer?
4. What product/service are you selling to resolve this customer issue?
5. If you are right how far can this idea go in terms of duplicating the idea?
6. How Getoutable is this business for you personally?
7. What are you banking on being right?

8.6. The 7 Fences

Orange Kangaroo now provides you with 7 Fences. 7 key areas which have to ALL align for you to have a successful new venture idea. Consider each in turn. Be sombre and without emotion – like the Vulcan-no sentiment Orange Kangaroo.

At the end of each Fence Concept ask yourself

"Which of these best describes my business idea against this fence test?"

Cleared (You go on to the next Fence)

Failed (You go back to see Yellow Kangaroo in Chapter 7 – this is Professional)

Swivel Point (if you have a swivel point you need to start to 7 Fences again)

Exercise – you will find a grid at the end of this Chapter which Orange Kangaroo has prepared for you. It will allow you to record your position at each of the 7 Fences.

Fence 1. Who is the Customer who has the money to spend?

Take note …. To Spend. Not customers who like the idea. No. Customers with money to BUY your product or service. To BUY it.

Do you know exactly what this customer looks like?

The best thing here is to think about a persona. Then build a collage profile just like the detectives do when chasing a criminal. Physically build up a "wall board" of this customer. Make them a real person that would be your customer. You might want to clip a photo of someone who looks like your customer appears to you in your head.

Create a customer profile.

Give them a name, an age, what they like, don't like. Their family situation.

Their ability to spend, their job, salary, routine.

Really build this up fully. End up with at least an A4 sheet or image on your PC. But a whole wall is much better.

You can do the same in a B2B situation too.

It may be a group of people in this instance, but the same principle applies. Again build a persona collage. Every customer you envisage needs a photo.

- Who are they?
- What do they do?
- What are their roles?
- How do they interact together?

Many of you reading this as experienced business people know lots about profiling. Orange Kangaroo does not want to make this element tedious.

But he does have the following advice, which I think has merit.

1. Don't segment you market and come up with multiple target customer profiles. This will dilute your edge and product testing process. Go for a single customer type and get them 100% clear in your mind. No 150% clear is better.

2. Don't profile B2B customers that buy through tendering. Tendering has killed off more SME's than cancer. It is lethal to start-ups. Customers who buy through tendering are SO unpredictable that you cannot profile your start up on this basis. The politicos will frown at this, but Orange Kangaroo is a Vulcan he does not care. His only job is to protect you Bouncepreneur.

Leave tendering for the HugeCorp that buys your business from you, after it has made you rich.

Now complete your 7 Fences summary exercise at the end of this Chapter.

Fence 2. How Many like them are there?

This question will tell you how much you can Scale Up your business idea is. As you know well by now building a business that can scale up without a large increase in costs is central to the Bouncepreneur ideal.

You cannot become Rich if your business does not scale up. This is essential. So you must know how many customers that fit your profile are out there.

This is no time for blind hope.

A quick word on scalability at this point. There are three forms of model regarding scalability worth thinking about.

Much thinking on scalability comes from businesses who are looking for investors. The common thinking being that without investors your idea will be overtaken by competition before it reaches a critical scale for you to get rich.

I say this, if your business is good the investors will show themselves. Better still you build it up from accelerating cash flow.

Type A Software/e Publishing

This type of business scales up quickly with low additional costs for every new customer. That is why it is so very popular as a Money Engine.

Type B Retail

This business scales less quickly, but can still move fast. Plus, reminds Orange Kangaroo Guide each retail unit can generate very significant income. However costs do rise as your chain grows. But if your service and product model is of a really high quality, you will be able to scale. Take the Chinese Buffet in the UK, well on the way to becoming the first national chain of Chinese Buffets. The first of its type despite significant competition from all sorts of eateries both chains and independents.

So when you are asking the "How Many Are There" question in this scenario also ask – How Many towns/cities can I set up in where my customer profile exists in numbers.

Type C Factory

Too many people dismiss manufacturing as too capital intensive to start and scale. But this is not true. If you see a Krones Canmatic labelling machine whizzing through bottles of sauce, whisky, sparkling water or soup cans at 600 per minute you will see a money machine before your very eyes.

You are resourceful Bouncepreneur. You may not be able to buy a new Canmatic – but there are alternatives – contract packing for example. The revival of marvellous Wrexham Lager – found on the Titanic uses a contract packager.

So when you are thinking about scalability in a manufactured product, you can still think about your customers – even in FMCG goods like sauce and soup.

The key here is how many customers are available to you that match your customer profile and persona.

For example, if the market you are trying to evaluate is for a new form of ready meal for elderly customers in your town. You may need to estimate the number of first level assumptions could look something like this:

- Number of infirm elderly people in your town?
- How many of these potential customers are catered for by the state?
- Have special dietary requirements?

Now complete your 7 Fences summary exercise at the end of this Chapter.

FENCE 3. What Issue Are You Solving For Your Customer? Your Bankable Assumption

Identify the right problem. This is critical: you must try to solve the right problem.

Orange Kangaroo calls this the Bankable Assumption. It is the one statement which defines the issue you are solving and the whole of the business idea sits on.

A good example is BuildaBear. This business idea sits on the Bankable Assumption that parents would pay quite a lot of money to let their kids buy and dress up a bear in a store. This is a Bankable Assumption that has worked.

I myself spent two years trying to solve the problem of benchmarking between contact centres only to solve a problem the customer saw as a nice to know, but not worth spending real money on. But if we had put the same effort into workforce management software we would have had a huge hit on our hands. My Bankable Assumption was plain wrong.

You must make sure that you are identifying the BIG issue by asking great questions and very careful observation.

Orange Kangaroo says it is worth remembering that according to the Harvard Business Review 67 percent of customers who leave a supplier say they were happy before they moved. So watch very carefully, as customers can mislead – especially over buying intentions. A basic questionnaire is nowhere near good enough.

Whatever you do don't put your core issue questions to friends and family. It is a recipe for disaster – they love you too much to say no. Bless them!

Both B2B and retail consumers are bombarded with choices every day of the year. Yours is not special.

Remember put your brainpower into building a MUST HAVE and not a NICE TO HAVE.

Interrogate

- What's leading the customer to feel there is a problem?
- Is it the issue real and specific or simply perceived to be a problem?
- Can the customer themselves define the problem? Ask and see what they say!
- How long does the problem last?
- Does it come back if untreated?
- Does is get bigger over time?
- Can the problem hurt people or a company?
- How easy the problem is to solve?

Passion

Now what I am going to say next won't please everybody. Especially HugeCorp.

Your business should NOT be your passion.

Many entrepreneurs seek to solve customer problems they identify with or feel passionate about. Many love their product and do not have a solid Bankable Assumption.

WRONG, WRONG, WRONG – especially at Bounce Back.

People who do this choose are more about enjoying the work than making money.

In the Bouncepreneur model YOU WON'T BE DOING THE WORK! Not for long at least. Passion makes people choose business ideas from the heart and not the head. Don't be one of these.

- That twee little bookstore to read to children – Closed
- The gym that no-one goes to because the location choice was so poor – GONE
- The small boat builder that cannot win a Navy tender due to poor credit ratings ADIOS

Now complete your 7 Fences summary exercise at the end of this Chapter.

FENCE 4. What product/service are you selling to resolve this customer issue?

Does your product find new customer need or pain? OR

Does your product reinvent something that has faded from the market for a long gone reason?

Here Orange Kangaroo asks you to clearly define your product/service in less than 20 words. If you struggle to describe it in 20 words it may lack clarity.

My product or service is

_____
_____

Now complete your 7 Fences summary exercise at the end of this Chapter.

FENCE 5. If you are right how far can this idea go?

Now if you are right, and the idea you are betting on being bankable comes to pass you have another question to consider

HOW FAR CAN THIS IDEA GO?

It can be a great idea. But how far can it go really?

Bouncepreneurs go for scale. So you have to be pre-prepared to go for scale. To smooth off the rough edges as soon as the customers have bitten and proven the model. Then you grow the business – fast1

That is what you really need to think about when planning your business.

I tried to establish a specialist sports holiday business. It marketed holidays in lots of locations and took a percentage of the booking fee. The model worked to some extent. Sales started to trickle in. But there was no surge of revenue. No Scale Up.

I decided to pull the annual returns on the biggest player in my market. The biggest player in the world. I soon saw that this business had the turnover and margins of a retail travel agency in a single town. It had been in business for 20 years!

It was in short, a lifestyle business. Albeit the market leader. Furthermore, volatile political situations in several of its key destinations were playing havoc with its income.

I looked at my own business, which was in effect a copycat idea and saw that my business idea had nowhere to go. It could neither replicate nor scale up.

I wasted a year! My idea failed the Scale Up test.

So at the planning stage you must ask yourself the question HOW FAR CAN THIS IDEA GO?

Here are a selection of Orange Kangaroo Guide's probing statements from a range of business type, see how they fit with your idea and try to come up with some of your own.

- This idea can be sold online around the world
- It can work in many languages
- It can be manufactured and sold on an industrial scale
- Would every town of more than 20,000 people support one of these retail units
- Contract packaging allows this idea to be ramped up in multiple countries
- Licensing the idea to gym chains allows this idea to ramp up rapidly
- Franchising is a way to rapidly expand the business concept

The main thing to think about is that to ramp up, it will not be you working around the clock to keep up with rocketing demand.

You need to see the opportunity to ramp up rapidly after launch and how you can achieve this. As a Professional Entrepreneur you have to expect your idea to work and demand to be high.

Now complete your 7 Fences summary exercise at the end of this Chapter.

Fence 6. How Getoutable is this business for you personally?

On the basis that you have a business which is growing rapidly, you have to be able to get out of operations altogether within 6 months, or a year at the absolute maximum.

I hear HugeCorp scoffing. But Orange Kangaroo plainly states it is achievable and highly desirable.

This is why you will never have a Getoutable business if you are doing work yourself. You have to delegate within 3 months.

Imagine four large, strong Kangaroos. All of them smart, efficient, personable. Think of Sergeant Majors. Think of your Kangaroo with stripes on their arms. These Sergeant Majors will allow you to get out of your business operations within a year.

They will:-

- Follow your plan
- Ensure your future workers follow your plan
- Run a well-oiled machine
- Report to you clearly and cleanly
- Embrace being part of the tribe you have created and respect you for it

To do this your business has to have clear areas of responsibility. These are

- Operations – the doing, making and distribution
- Finance and Administration
- Sales & Marketing
- Customer Service & Feedback

Each one of these roles you will do first, when you launch your venture. You will establish procedures fully and then hand them over to a replacement in each of these areas over the first 6 months of your new business' life.

Orange Kangaroo reminds you without emotion, that if you have not got the revenue flow to do this, then your business has failed and you have failed to test it thoroughly enough before launch. It will require a major Swivel Point or to be closed.

What this means for you is a long period of being broke and being enslaved to a horrible job of long hours and probably poor money. Orange Kangaroo is sure you do not want this.

As part of your business plan DO write job descriptions for the four roles listed above.

Remember you have not developed this business idea to be ripped up or diluted by your staff.

Recruit your Kangaroo Sergeant-Major on this basis

- She or he already has the skills in the area you need
- He/she will deliver your plan
- They will stick to your plan and understand the need for focus NOT disruption
- He/she can work to a quarterly plan without you
- They can recruit the people in their area without you

Within a year you will replace yourself as Managing Director of this business. You then become its main investor.

Now complete your 7 Fences summary exercise at the end of this Chapter.

FENCE 7. The Super Fence - Your Bankable Assumption

This fence is the most important one of all. What are you banking on being right? So we call it the Super Fence.

There will be one key bet (Bankable Assumption) you are gambling on being right which will depend on the success or failure of your venture. It is that simple!

Let's start with a great example.

In the USA a small airplane company called Boomsupersonic. They intend to fly a small version of Concorde with just 45 passengers between New York and London.

They are banking on passengers being prepared to pay three times more for a ticket to get across much faster.

For me, it they are banking on a very likely customer need. Wealthy business people and Stars like Joan Collins adored the old Concorde because it allowed them to commute faster and get more done. Ask a retired travel agent his or her most remarkable experience. Travelling on Concorde will be right up there.

Here's a really simple example

Take this book. I myself am banking on the fact that there are lots of entrepreneurs needing help to overcome their loss of belief in being both Rich and Happy.

Now a flawed example

A friend of mine Mark is planning to import a new type of photograph that goes onto a grave stone. The photograph does not fade in the sun like existing ones. He is banking on families seeing this as important.

However, when he told me about this idea, my thoughts were different. I thought having lost a loved one, families would be taking advice from their Funeral Director, picking the right photograph. Picking a process for the photograph's manufacture might not register as important.

I saw the recommendation of the Funeral Director as the critical bankable feature here as this person is often known to and respected by the family.

Think About These Examples Yourself

Here are some examples from entrepreneurs I have spoken to. Which of these do you think are Bankable and worth betting a year of your life on being right?

- People will see our honey in the same way the see Manuka honey
- Portuguese people like to drink coffee in a café which reminds them of home
- There is no Health and Safety software where the emphasis is placed on the worker to sign off understanding of the issues relating to specific tasks that day

- Customers will see that voice automation is more secure in terms of customer data than offshoring
- Students will love a low cost electric motorbike
- Entrepreneurs will see the benefits of a bank account with built in bookkeeping software

Now what KEY BET are you banking on being right? Think hard and make sure you KNOW you are right.

If you have doubts about your Bankable Assumption this is ok. If you test your idea further and find ANY Fence is looking like it cannot be cleared. You can perform a Swivel Turn. Imagine yourself as the Kangaroo unable to jump the Fence. So you turn left or right (you modify your ideas and assumptions) until you find a point to jump the fence OR a gap in it.

But you may not find the right opportunity, meaning you do not have a bankable assumption. This is ok. It means you go back to Yellow Kangaroo as a Professional Entrepreneur and come up with another product or service idea entirely.

Now complete your 7 Fences summary exercise at the end of this Chapter.

YOUR 7 FENCES SUMMARY EXERCISE

FENCE	FENCE NAME & YOUR DESCRIPTION	ACID TEST QUESTIONS & YOUR ANSWER	Go forward Abandon Swivel Point
Customer	Who is the customer with money to spend?	How do you know they have this money?	
Number	How many like them are there?	How do you know there are X many like them?	
Issue	What issue are you solving for your customer?	How do you know this is an issue?	
Product	What product/service are you selling to solve this issue	How do you know this product will solve this issue?	
Duplicate	Can you duplicate this idea many times?	How can you duplicate this idea?	
Get Out	How Getoutable is this idea?	How can you get out within a year?	

Bankable Assumption	What are your betting on being right?		

Idea Decision
[ ] Abandon this Idea Completely Go Back to see Yellow Kangaroo for a Better Idea
[ ] Go Forward with This Idea to the Next Kangaroo Guide
[ ] Swivel Point – You need to make a change then retest your idea (detail the Swivel Point)
_____
_____
_____

8.7. Orange Kangaroo's Key Lessons

In this Chapter Orange Kangaroo has taught you to put your business idea through the most rigorous of tests. In his purely objective Spock-like personality, he has encouraged you to make THE most unbiased check on the validity of your business idea. He has given you the 7 Fences exercise to really test all aspects of your business idea.

He has shown you clearly that you have the opportunity as a Professional Entrepreneur to move back from his Orange Kangaroo stage back to Yellow Kangaroo, if you need his help to generate a better business idea.

Now it is time for Orange Kangaroo to hand you onto your next Kangaroo Guide who is Green Kangaroo. Green Kangaroo will make sure you that the product or service you launch does not hurt you too much if it fails to launch AND how to rapidly ramp up if the product does well.

I would suggest you say goodbye to Orange Kangaroo. But he has already gone. He never was one for niceties!

CONGRATULATIONS YOU ARE NOW AN ORANGE BELT BOUNCEPRENEUR

9. Green Kangaroo Bouncepreneur Minimum Viable Product

9.1. Green Kangaroo Introduction

Green Kangaroo bids you welcome to her Chapter which will guide you through the launch of your new product of service as a Minimum Viable Product (MVP) or Bouncepreneur MVP – BMVP.

She strongly recommends that you take her guidance on board along with that from your next two Guides Blue Kangaroo and Brown Kangaroo. This is very important.

You may benefit from reading all three Chapters in the same session.

Green Kangaroo will Guide you through a 30 day launching of your new product or service which is intended to offer you the lowest financial and time risk. Blue Kangaroo's Guidance will assist you in making an unconventional yet effective business plan to ride your new venture for the first 6 months. Finally Brown Kangaroo's guidance will give you real capability in meeting the 4 BIG challenges you will have to overcome to move the business from the first 30 days. Leading to a successful first six month mark and beyond.

Now Green Kangaroo will lead you in taking the idea that you have carefully assessed in the 7 Fences forward.

You may be interested in knowing a little more about Green Kangaroo. She really is very impressive. Green is the fastest Kangaroo Guide of them all. She is the ultimate business heptathlete - the Jessica Ennis-Hill of entrepreneurs. Although Green Kangaroo is fit, lean and built for sprinting, she is more than just speed, she has endurance, flexibility and competitive instinct. She is hugely capable, able to win at multiple disciplines in an intense period of effort.

This is why Green Kangaroo makes the perfect Kangaroo Guide for launching a new business, quickly and effectively. She knows many ways to cross the 30 Day Launch Period finish line as a winner.

Yes you read right you are going to successfully launch your new business idea within 30 days. At the end of 30 days you will also have at the very least a salary.

Green Kangaroo first reminds you that as a Professional Entrepreneur you still want to ensure that the venture you immerse yourself into is DEFINITELY GOING TO WORK. If despite all your testing the idea does not take off Green will ensure you do not lose your shirt in terms of time or cash.

She will do this by means of the Bouncepreneur Minimum Viable Product Model. (BMVP)

You will launch your new idea with explosive energy of course. But Green Kangaroo wants to make sure you spend as little money as possible live testing your business venture.

So in summary, figuring out whether what you're building is something people want.

You are going to test your business idea as a live business

But if it works

YOU ARE GOING TO RUN LIKE HELL WITH IT!

9.2. BMVP Further Explained

Green Kangaroo is a huge fan of Bear Grylls the Chief Scout, famous adventurer and survivor. Well aren't we all in fact!

She asks you to think of your business launch in the same way Bear builds a fire.

He prepares very carefully.

With care he finds his tinder and lays it out in front of him. He seems to use just a tiny amount of inflammable material.

He already has a pre-prepared pile of very thin twigs right next to him.

Next to these are slightly bigger twigs

And then a few big branches.

He carefully rubs his sticks together to get a spark on his tinder.

Then once he sees the smallest flames in his tinder, he blows on the fire, but then he has he small twigs right next to him which he can reach straight away.

When these light he has his next biggest twigs, again right next to him

And then when the fire is established on goes the big logs. Yes these are there pre-prepared too.

When Bear has spark making a tiny fire, does he have to find some small twigs? No. They are ready.

When his small twigs are alight does he go off to get some branches? Again No. He has them.

Bear wants his fire to Explode into life – just like your business idea.

Once the fire lights he has everything ready. AND so must you when your idea catches light. You must have everything right next to you to make it work immediately.

And if Bear has tinder that is wet and won't take a spark what does he do?

He does not spend 12 hours trying to light it.

No. He makes an intense, skilful effort. But if it doesn't want to light no useless effort is made.

Bear either throws the useless tinder away, sleeps cold and finds some new the next day.

Green Kangaroo tells you:-

- You have to have great tinder – your idea
- You need to prepare everything you need to make a great fire from the tiniest of sparks
- It is all about preparation
- If unexpectedly you find your tinder is no good. You acknowledge it and sleep cold. But you don't flog a dead horse.

In the BMVP model you have a 30 Day Rolling Start to get your business blazing.

If your tinder (idea) catches light you will go from testing your business idea to straight to actually trading. For real. Straight in.

Your goal – a month's salary.

But if the venture does not achieve success, you are going to build the launch so that it does not over commit you, the Professional Entrepreneur to a terminal failure.

9.3. Avoid, Avoid, Avoid the Old Way of Launching a Business

Green Kangaroo places her hands on her hips and laughs out loud as she asks you to think about the old-school way of launching a business. Entrepreneurs completed their huge irrelevant business plan, which once they launched their business just gathered dust for years.

The old way was minted by HugeCorp, but was terrible for a Bouncepreneur or other start up with limited or no capital.

She shakes her head sadly thinking too many people are still educated to plan for investment that your product testing does not justify.

Don't go this way Bouncepreneur says Green Kangaroo.

In the past you may have committed fully to the LAUNCH of your new business on Day 1. For example you may have:-

- Rented an office, shop or factory
- Bought capital equipment or a full barista coffee machine or chairs for 4 hair stylists
- Recruited staff
- Sunk in all your savings
- Borrowed from the bank

If this method works out great. If it does not, then you have another failure and maybe years of debt on your hands.

9.4. BMVP A Better Way

Nobody wants a failed project for you, especially Green Kangaroo because she has a huge heart for Bounce Backs.

Green Kangaroos limit the duration of your launch phase to 30 days. If it works out you go forward. If the venture fails you revert back to earlier Phases maybe needing more work on your idea or an alternative.

Green Kangaroo has three main objectives for her Students.

1. To minimise your investment in taking your product to market
2. To allow you to know within 30 days whether you have a hit or not
3. To show that you can build a test process that is not just a light bite test of your idea, but it can be your full business roll out too.

The 30 Day Green Kangaroo Phase is so valuable to Bouncepreneurs because most of you are bouncing back on a shoe-string. This approach encourages the most basic, low cost form of the product you can possibly launch.

The idea of trying a "Light Bite" version of a full product before committing resources to actually doing it, is not new - Housebuilders been doing it for years. Buying off plan as it is called is commonplace. Especially so if the properties are going to be in high demand. Often when houses or especially apartments/flats are built the builder will market the properties to potential buyers before the first home is even started.

If nobody wants to buy, the builder does not build. It is that simple.

Vendors use computerised and real models to demonstrate what the property might look like and provide samples for floor tiles, kitchen layouts and paint schemes.

So why can't you do this with your product or service?

9.5. What You Have to Do Bouncepreneur?

According to Green Kangaroo you have to do 6 things to deliver this launch:-

1. You have to build the most basic/low cost version of your product or service you can.
2. You have to do this within 90 days from the idea and 7 Fence Test
3. You must remember you are doing this to find out IF customers will buy it.
4. <u>Not</u> customers might buy it if you tweak A, B and C but they will buy what you have NOW!
5. You have to sell enough of this product within 30 days of launch to pay yourself a salary
6. If the idea works and sales flow in, you start the business for real.

Here are some additional considerations Green Kangaroo suggests you think about

FURTHER CONSIDERATIONS

- A product that you are able to demonstrate in full to the point of asking for money
- It must work or appear to work for demonstration purposes
- It has to be bought within 30 days by a predetermined number of customers
- You need a marketing strategy to complement the launch
- It has to be bought right now. Promises of purchase in the future do not count. Binding orders and cash only.
- The customer clearly likes it
- The customer sees it solves the problem you designed it for
- The customer loves your product and buys it, but to solve a different problem than you envisaged
- It must be a better solution to the customer's problem than anything else they have used before
- It must be a better solution to the customer's problem
- Build the business as a web site
- Remember you don't have to sell it to everybody
- Remember some people who never buy it even if you Gold Plate it and offer it for free
- Have your marketing and operations ready to go and ramp up at a moment's notice.
- A single idea – no customisations for individual customers – no matter how tempting

9.6. How to Build a BMVP

Some Ways to Build a Bouncepreneur Minimum Viable Product (BMVP)

Green Kangaroo has several ideas to help you build a BMVP.

Video Explainer - You simply make a video explainer. This can be done very inexpensively now and you capture sales orders or sales enquiries at the end of the video.

Early Adopter Exclusivity - If you are supplying a fairly big ticket market with perhaps 10 competitors you offer your new product to just three for one year. You present a mock up but say that you will only be working with three "Foundation Partners."

This is especially useful if you sell internationally. You have your anchor clients to use as sales case studies but in every other country you sell to all the customers. In the second year you do the same in your local market.

Concierge - In this model you basically promise the customer a service and then once they have ordered you do all the work needed yourself to ensure they get the service they are paying for. Now you would kill yourself doing this for any length of time, but to prove the concept it is a good approach.

Effectively you make nothing up front.

Wizard of Oz - In the Wizard of Oz a frail old man made outsiders believe he was huge, powerful and almost Godlike with all sorts of trickery.

Well you can do the same projecting a bigger version of your business than you actually are – be careful not to lie. Lying is bad business and bad Karma.

Restricted Product or Service - Offer a "Basic" version of your product. One which you can make or provide easily. Then later you can add whistles and bells and increase the price.

Obviously very popular in software, but it can be used in hospitality, furniture business and even car washing.

When I worked for a car parts company, many moons ago we market tested brand name for spark plugs and other service parts for cars. The tradition was to use the term Bronze, Silver and Gold for these items. Most competitors used the same terms.

We changed the approach introducing the term STANDARD instead of Bronze. It was the same product. Sales rose. Because people wanted just that, an inexpensive Standard product.

3D Printed - 3D printing allows manufacturing minded entrepreneurs to build one off examples of what they have in mind for customers. These can be photographed or shown as videos or physical shown to customers.

You can go to 3D printers with buying your own device for one off designs. It is a great idea to launch products.

You Show an Existing Competitors Product - You can show a competitors product and point out deficiencies it has. You can show customers how you have improved on these deficiencies and that the customer can buy this improved version from you now.

Scale Mock ups - You might use 3D printing for this too. Alternatively if you were planning to build a fairground ride for example you could build a scale replica to close the order on. Remember you do not need the full size product to seal your first deals.

Payable Demo - Here you are really selling the idea. You are saying you can see the idea we have, but you must pay to be in the room.

This can be tricky and impossible in my view if you are selling to government. But if you have a radical idea it can be done.

I have seen it done in packaging where customers were told that there would be limited supply for a year, but a new product would cut costs VERY significantly for the customer. Because some of these customers were known to be loyal to competitors a payable demo was insisted on. It worked very well, because the supplier was genuinely able to deliver huge savings and the customers were receptive having a problem that no one had yet fully solved.

9.7. Make Buying From You Easy

You may have a great product or service. You have found a need and have a solution the customer wants. But do not make buying difficult for the customer!

Green Kangaroo suggests you bear these points in mind.

Keep it Simple – Do not bring a complex idea to market. Make sure customers are able to understand it VERY, VERY easily.

No Handcuffs - offer a service that customers can leave if they wish. Do not try to create contractual conditions that are long and very binding. If a customer thinks they can leave easily then they are far more likely to relax and buy.

Trayable – just make sure the customer can try the product really easily. Do not make them perform tricks just to get a chance to try it. They will not thank you for it.

Longevity – try to make the product or service you are offering more than just a one deal wonder. Find ways to entice the customer to stay with you for a long time.

Very Simple to Buy – A mistake Green Kangaroo says happens all the time and can kill a launch venture is making the e-commerce or simple payment process too complicated. The customer wants to buy, but you cannot take credit cards or you cannot accept an invoice. Even at the Green Kangaroo Phase make sure you give the customer the most ways you can to pay. Sure it is a lot of work. Set something reasonable up. For sure it can actually be very time consuming and fiddly, but it is worth it and what Professional Entrepreneurs do.

9.8. Questions from Real-Life Bouncepreneurs

Green Kangaroo now shares a series of questions that have been asked by real life Bouncepreneurs at this stage of the process.

Question – What if it does not work out in 30 days?

- If you REALLY feel a small change can make all the difference you modify and try again, but for no more than an additional 30 days
- If the idea doesn't work you abandon it entirely at the end of the month and go back to see Yellow Kangaroo about alternative ideas

Green Kangaroo emphasises your product has to be MINIMALISTIC

This product has to be a basic as it can be. But people will buy it as it stands.

It does not have to be a full working version, but you need to be able to deliver it ethically.

Question – What if it really takes off?

You need to have the process, job roles and tasks to deliver set up in advance.

If it takes off you must be ready to roll and handle the volume

Question – What timescales are you recommending?

- You have 30 days from Day 1 of launch to sell this product or service.
- If you cannot sell it to point of cash payment or purchase order the launch has failed.
- If you really feel a Turning Point adjustment will see this idea lift off then give the venture 30 more days. But do not carry on with the venture if you do not see revenue. Don't do it.
- You have 90 days to prepare the product for launch. If it takes longer do not do it.

Question – How Should I Demonstrate My Product or Service

You have to be able to demonstrate your product effectively from Day 1 of launch

This can be a physical product, but can also be a simulation ranging from a CAD mock-up, non-functioning website, video presentation or scale model. 3D printing really opens up this method.

Your demonstration is a sales demonstration – pure and simple – you are there to close on this product sale.

You must make certain money promised to you in sales hit your bank account. Until it is in your bank it does not count.

Question – How Much Variation Should I Offer

The short answer is as little as possible.

You should not accept orders for one off variations, design modifications for single customers. If you do this says Green Kangaroo you are winning one sale at the cost of proving your business model.

Keep any ranges you need as limited as possible.

Question – Is it Ethical to Offer a Product You Cannot Deliver?

You must be able to deliver the product or service you have demonstrated and taken money for.

To do anything else is not ethical.

Now it might take you a while to deliver, but so long as you have not duped or misled the customer this is ok.

Quite a few people in retail and B2B markets enjoy being early adopters very much indeed!

Question – How Much Money Should I Spend On This

Green Kangaroo has a simple answer to this. AS LITTLE AS POSSIBLE. You must build this launch version based on what you can afford. It may just take your time and computer.

It may take other resources that you have at your disposal.

You must think micro budget.

Do not deplete your resources on building sophisticated prototypes. If your idea needs £50,000 to build, find a way of mocking it up virtually.

Do not blow all your savings. Be a Professional Entrepreneur reminds the Green Kangaroo Guide, you may need to abandon this idea and try another.

Question – How do I Judge a Successful Launch?

You must make a salary by the end of your launch month. It may not be a big salary but you must make one.

You must see that month 2 is going to pay you very well

Month 3 your Money Engine is firing really well enough to recruit

Question – Do I Look for Investors or Take Out a Bank Loan

No you do not. You do not look for investors on your first Bounce Back business. You may do this on your second or third venture. But ideally you will self-fund you next business from this one.

If your business idea demands external investment from the start, don't do it. Go back to Yellow Kangaroo and come up with a more modest plan. Remember your first Bounce Back business needs to be a hit. It is better for it to be successful and small, than unsuccessful and big.

HugeCorp Dingoes have told us that you cannot launch a business without capital from them. They repeat ad nausea that you should be scared of:-

- Legal Issues
- Fear of Idea Theft
- Fear of Rejection

Green Kangaroo is defiant and says get the revenue flowing and take it from there.

If you spend a small amount to check the validity of an idea you can still go again. If you invest heavily and it fails – well you are broke for a really long time.

Question – Do I have to wait for Day 1 Before Starting Sales and Marketing

Now get going – emphasises Green Kangaroo. You must give yourself every advantage possible.

- You need a website able to support your sales messages so get busy
- Start telling people in your target market about your new product before you launch it
- Build expectation for your product
- You must be able to take payments on the basis customers are likely to want to pay you.
- Your website must be able to handle payments, get working on this

Question – How much preparation do I need to do for the business really taking off?

Lots - is the answer Green Kangaroo offers

- This is a rolling start business. That means you must have a ramp up plan ready
- You need to be prepared to rapidly fulfil orders, outsource non-essentials and build product
- You have to have your processes and the beginnings of job descriptions for your Kangaroo Sergeant Majors ready.

Question – How good must the quality of my product be?

- Your product or service must be the most basic design you can come up with capable of supporting an ethical sale.
- The quality of your product (although simple) must be good
- You will be able to quickly improve the quality and polish of your product once sales start

Question – How much of a research versus sales process is this?

Green Kangaroo hates this question. You see her bristling when it is asked. She was once overheard being asked by a HugeCorp consultant

"What is the best method you have for successfully launching a product?" to which Green Kangaroo answered

"If doesn't matter does it! Because you'll know a better one!"

Her advice to Bouncepreneurs is simple. This process can give you great understanding of your customer AND give you're a great launch OR it can give you a great understanding of your customer AND save you lots of time and expense if it does not launch well.

Question – Should one think of this as a Research Exercise

Yes in part. But Green Kangaroo shows us why she is so competitive and the fastest Kangaroo of all. She emphasises that if you go into a product launch without a total commitment to closing business you are in deep trouble. She advises:-

- Put on your sales hat
- Come with your A sales game
- Be ready to hustle for business

You will HOWEVER, be able to get other useful information on customer preference.

Question – In What Situation Should I Change My Product on the Hoof

Most successful businesses see a Swivel Point necessity during or shortly after launch. Green Kangaroo emphasises the need to be clear on bespoke customisation and a majority of customers showing a need for a revised product.

She suggests the following approach.

If one person asks you to change your product this is a customisation. Two customers ask, then this is still a customisation to be avoided. But if a big chunk of people you try to sell to, keep asking for the same modification, then you should do it. If you know you can make this change, then change your mock up or demo and sell it with the change.

Make it happen. But the Golden Rule is to close the deal, even using the initial design.

"I will change it if you buy it now." Is a good mantra says Green Kangaroo. Here is a real example.

A Bouncepreneur called Martina manufactured samples of toddler clothes and tried to sell them to the mums she knew from her local kindergarten and playgroups in her area. This lady was from Slovakia and had used complex hand wash only trimmings were well know and liked in her home country.

But she now lived in the UK and tastes were very different. Many prospective buyers said to her that if the fabrics were more washable they would buy. So our Bouncepreneur made up some fabric swatches and sold her clothes using her original ornate garments with the new more washable fabrics on her swatches. After she could see this was viable and people were actually buying she went back to her sewing machine. Like a Bouncepreneur Cinderella she worked really hard to make the same garments in the requested fabrics. This time they sold and they sold really well. In fact they were so successful she was asked by her local nursery Kindergarten to provide these as the official uniform for pre-schoolers.

Martina then made a second Turning Point. She took the idea of Kindergarten uniforms to other pre-schools and now her core business is making pre-school children's clothes for Kindergartens.

Question – What if I Simply Cannot Find Enough Customers in 30 Days

If you have not pitched the product or service to at least 10 customers in your target market with the issue you seek to solve you have not completed a successful launch. Either because your sales and marketing effort has lacked bite OR…

You may have not completed Yellow and Orange Kangaroo's work properly and you never did have enough customers to support your idea at all.

Question – What about a "Failed Launched"

Green Kangaroo sets the record straight when she says there is no such thing as a failure in this process.

Your launch has failed, but you have succeeded in terms of safeguarding yourself from a potentially ruinous venture.

9.9. You Are Unable to Sell Your Product or Service

Firstly if the launch does not work out pull the product launch at the end of thirty days. You have to retreat and rethink.

Be sure to contact all customers who you have taken or progressing orders with and explain openly and honestly what has happened. Refund all monies not owed to you. Apologise sincerely for the inconvenience. People are amazing in this situations. It is important to do this because the same people may become your customers for a revised product launch in the future.

Green Kangaroo encourages you to remember 4 key things.

- You are acting as a Professional Entrepreneur NOT a Failure
- The learning will allow you to go back to the 7 Fences and be even more Professional in your approach
- You have saved a huge amount of time, effort and money compared with a less organised venture launch. You have progressed.
- Do not be downbeat

If the launch fails, think like a Professional Entrepreneur not an Amateur Entrepreneur. Once you become a serial Entrepreneur you will accept some failure in product launch as part of the risk process.

So pull the product and review the experience carefully.

If you feel there is merit in a rebuild of your product, take it back to Yellow Kangaroo. Let her shine some light on the experience. You may decide there is some opportunity worth salvaging OR you should totally abandon the idea.

If you need to swivel turn left or right and find another gap in the fence that is ok. Better than, than to waste months of your life and your very limited capital and confidence.

9.10 Green Kangaroo's Key Lessons

Green is the most dynamic of all the Kangaroo's.

Although you have previously tested your idea for soundness at the Orange Kangaroo Guide's 7 Fences, Green Kangaroo has sought to protect you from failure. She has done this by showing you a safer, yet expandable product launch process - Bouncepreneur Minimum Viable Product (BMVP). This sits between testing and full roll out. It gives an opportunity to be sure of success and a real-life launch AS WELL AS the opportunity to retreat/rethink without blowing all your money.

Now you are going for a final stage of testing where you are selling in earnest.

Green Kangaroo insists at launch you make your first month's salary.

Green has also taught you:-

- You launch a Light Bite version of your product or service at minimal costs. A "Good Enough" product.
- You only offer a product or service ethically that you can deliver in some way to the quality promised.
- You will have a ramp up plan ready to roll if the product tests well.
- If the product tests well you go for a rapid ramp up with all your effort.
- If the product does not achieve a sales within 30 days, you either, make an objective Swivel Point modification and try again for a further 30 days OR you pull the idea completely and go back to the Orange or even Yellow Kangaroo Guides for a rethink.
- You do not spend money you do not have on this process.
- You do not spend more than 90 days developing the idea prior to launch.

- If your idea lifts off you will need to have a series of resources and plans ready.

In the upcoming two Chapters you will meet your next Guides, first Blue Kangaroo and then Brown Kangaroo.

Now it is time to say goodbye to Green Kangaroo. As is her nature she congratulates you equally warmly whether your product launch has taken off, or needs rework. Her final encouragement to you is to stay focussed on your goal and to enjoy some exercise. Success and Happiness.

With that Green Kangaroo bounces off – at tremendous speed of course.

CONGRATULATIONS YOU ARE NOW A GREEN BELT BOUNCEPRENEUR

Chapter 10 Blue Kangaroo Dance Around the Dingoes

10.1. Introduction

In this chapter you will meet your Blue Kangaroo Guide. He is quite a wolfish looking character. If there was ever a carnivorous Kangaroo it is your Blue Kangaroo Guide.

Now Blue Kangaroo looks like a corporate banker, always wearing a sharp, expensive dark blue pinstripe suit. In fact Blue Kangaroo used to be as HugeCorp as HugeCorp could be. But when he was made redundant by his employer of 30 years, he suffered a massive fall in living standards. Nowadays he gets his kicks from helping Bouncepreneurs understand how to dance around the HugeCorp Dingoes.

Blue Kangaroo is in his early fifties and at first site is a stranger to the gym. But what he lacks in physical fitness he makes up for with his huge laugh and zest for life. He loves helping Bouncepreneurs.

Twice a week Blue Kangaroo drags him to the swimming pool for his exercise. Although he would never admit it, he is a really strong swimmer these days.

But what Blue Kangaroo specialises in helping Bouncepreneurs with and what makes him such a formidable ally is his advice in planning and finance. Blue Kangaroo will tell you what you have to know to avoid getting caught out by the Dingoes as well as the financial controls that will make your business strong.

Blue Kangaroo has a healthy disdain towards HugeCorp. But he knows how to play the game and more importantly will guide you to have the best possible real-world financial control you need to reach success and happiness.

10.2. What You Need in Terms of Plans

Now you do of course need a business plan to take you from the start of your business with you BMVP launch to the end of a 6 month period. That's right a 6 month period! Not a 12 month period.

At the end of 6 months you will have Scaled Up and Duplicated your business and it will be time for you to Get Out of Operations.SUDGO

10.3. The Format of the Blue Kangaroo Plan

In recent times the traditional business plan, which we thoroughly lampooned earlier, is being replaced with some useful new thinking such as the Canvas Business Model.

But your Blue Kangaroo Guide does not want you to use this process and this is his rational.

a. He wants your plans to support the core principles of becoming a Bouncepreneurs, in that your business exists to be your Money Machine.

b. He does not want you working daily in this business after 6 months.

c. He does not want you to use investors to fund your business. Your first Bounce Back business may be very small. It will fund your second and third ventures. NOT big borrowing.

d. After all we have been through together in this book, Blue Kangaroo does not want to bring your Bouncepreneur Journey to conclusion with old school, HugeCorp thinking business planning.

e. Blue Kangaroo wants your business plan to follow Scale Up, Duplicate, Get Out (SUDGO) thinking.

10.4 Bouncepreneur's 10 Key Planning Principles

Blue Kangaroo has built up 10 Key Planning Principles.

10 Key Bouncepreneur Planning Principles

1. You must get a basic salary by the end of month one
2. You will pay yourself a really good salary at the end of month two
3. You must have total focus on customer need, quality and service. BUT you can be highly committed to your customer and service without being married to any one business
4. There are key targets you MUST ACHIEVE otherwise the business WILL fail.
5. There are four key planning and delivery areas SALES, DISCOVERABILITY, FACTORY, FAB (Finance, Admin & Bottlenecks)
6. You will use the Bouncepreneurs Plan for 6 months to deliver Success and Happiness.

7. You will also use and fully understand 3 TAD's Traditional Accounting Documents, Cash Flow Forecast, Balance Sheet, Profit & Loss Statement.
8. There are pre-set TRIGGERS to replace yourself in each of the four planning and delivery areas. Once these pre-sets are reached, you will replace yourself with one of four Kangaroo Sergeant Majors who can execute your plan as you have laid it out.
9. After month 6 you will take 20% of the businesses sales revenue (not profit) out to build you own personal NET WORTH – you will do this in addition to any salary you may draw.
10. Your fifth Sergeant-Major is the MD you will appoint to run the business. At this point you will become the Chairman.

10.5. Criticism You Will Hear from the Dingoes

Something Blue Kangaroo enjoyed writing for you. Here are a number of criticisms you may hear from the Dingoes about your plan. You will also see Blue Kangaroo's response. He is as stroppy and he is funny. But he knows how to help the Bouncepreneur streamline and run a lean operation for sure.

But below each one of these Blue Kangaroo (BK) wants you to write your own response. Be as irreverent as you want. Blue Kangaroo certainly is. Feel free to use your own language and style. No rules here at all.

But right at the end of this Chapter there is one more criticism for you to answer.

Criticism 1 The plan is too light – BK No it isn't!

Your Response

Criticism 2 It is too unconventional to work – BK Says Who are you again?

Your Response

Criticism 3 You will never get out of working in your business in 6 months – BK Watch me!

Your Response

Criticism 4 Investors won't like it – BK I don't need investors

Your Response

Criticism 5 There is no Budget and Actual – BK I only work on actual

Your Response

Criticism 6 What if it goes wrong? – BK Don't you mean what if it goes right!

Your Response

Criticism 7 You must have a full product before launch – BK Naaah! We are already selling, catch up!

Your Response

Criticism 8 A basic product is one thing but you'll never ramp up in time – BK Watch me!

Your Response

Criticism 9 You will run out of working capital – BK Your capital you mean! Nope!

Your Response

Criticism 10 You haven't written it from your audience perspective – BK Well you are wrong again!

Your Response

Criticism 11 What about the competitive analysis – BK I don't concern myself with that

Your Response

10.6. The Bouncepreneur Blue Kangaroo Business Planning Tool

In the Planning Tool which follows you will see a simple form for you to fill in.

- Complete the venture name
- Fill in a succinctly as possible the Customer Need you have found and intend to service
- Fill in the two salaries you will take after 30 and 60 days.
- Fill in launch date and 30, 60 and 180 dates, which are your key milestones.

As a reminder you will see you MUST ACHIEVE and MUST EVOLVE objectives.

Take a few minutes to digest these. Blue Kangaroo shows his teeth a little as he tells you these are MUST's.

Then we show your 5 management areas and for each a date when you will hand over the reins to a Sergeant Major who will run and build that department for you.

Finally you have scope for future problems you can see challenging your business.

There is also room for any planned solutions you may have in mind, but perhaps you cannot fund or are not sure how to overcome these future challenges.

But that is OK for now.

Bouncepreneur Blue Kangaroo Business Planning Tool

Venture Name

Customer Need:- After thorough testing and adjustment I have identified the following customer need which I will be fulfilling to create a Money Engine
Write Your Customer Need Here

Salary I will get at end of 30 days £/$/€_____	Salary I will get after 60 days £/$/€_____	
Launch Date __/__/__	30 Days Out __/__/__	60 Days Out __/__/__	180 Day GetOut __/__/__

Must Achieve Objectives

MUST ACHIEVE	MUST EVOLVE
1. Salary	1. Process Documentation
2. Discoverability	2. 5 Sergeants Job Descriptions
3. Sales Target	3. Financial Imperatives
4. Cost Control	4. Product Honing

Your Five Management Areas

SALES	DISCOVERY
Targets	Targets
Channels	Methods
Cost of Sales	Budgets
1st Sergeant Major Trigger Mth 3	2nd Sergeant Major Trigger Mth 4
FACTORY (work is done)	**F.A.B**
Process	Financial Control
Equipment	Administration
Materials	Buying
3rd Sergeant Major Trigger Mth 5	4th Sergeant Major Trigger Mth 6

5th Sergeant Major – Managing Director Month 7

Sales Discovery Factory F.A.B	

5 Future Problems	Planned Solutions
1.	
2.	
3.	
4.	
5.	

10.7 Blue Kangaroo's Control Method

Blue Kangaroo wants you to drive your first 6 months from launch with a Control Method and Not a Planning Method to ensure success.

What does this mean?

Well conventional planning advice has its merits – especially CASH FLOW and BREAK EVEN ANALYSIS. But much of the other stuff is all about

- Accountancy practices for larger firms
- Accounting convention
- Giving the Dingoes what they want in their little world
- Giving investors what they want
- Mimicking HugeCorp without asking why the hell are we doing this in this way
- Oh Yes and Your Tax Return!

Different Way of Doing This

Normally when you do your plan, your get told that the documents the Accountants use will help you build a successful business.

They won't.

But you HAVE to conform to the laws, tax and accounting regulations of your state.

So you have to get GOOD at accounting and book-keeping. You simply HAVE to. You cannot run a professional business without doing so.

Also you will be vulnerable to the Dingoes if you don't.

10.8 Scalable Duplicable GetOutable Dashboard (SDG)

Below you will see a simple dashboard and a few notes to explain it.

This dashboard is to help you stay on track to build a Scalable, Duplicable and Getoutable business.

Blue Kangaroo strongly recommends you print this out. Do it small and put it in your purse or wallet. But make a copy. At the end of each month fill in the boxes. You only need to write Yes or No. You do not put in numbers.

But you will really look forward to filling in these boxes BECAUSE you have worked so hard to FREE yourself and become rich and happy. Yes it is to help YOU become successful and happy. It is not for the tax man, bank, investor or anyone else. It is for you!

The purpose of this dashboard is for you to achieve three things once you have started:-

1. To make sure you hit those key goals
2. To make sure you get out of the business effectively
3. To make sure the business is focused on being a MONEY ENGINE

Blue Kangaroo reminds you that the Dingoes are going to look at this and be critical. Why? Because you are taking an unconventional path. For sure this 6 months is going to be hard and if you cannot make the Sales targets it won't work. That is why we tested SO thoroughly at the Orange Kangaroos 7 Fences and Green Kangaroo's BMVP Phases.

Your Personal SDG Dashboard							
Control/Month	1	2	3	4	5	6	7
All Yes or No Responses	Yes/No	Yes/No	Yes/No	Yes/No	Yes/No	Yes/No	Yes/No
Sales							
Costs							
Salary							
Profit							
20% to Net Worth							
Final Process Map							
Job Description							
Appointment							

Notes

i. Sales is your predetermined sales target that you need to achieve to achieve your salary, profit and net worth goal. Simply did you hit it or not? Costs, this is your fixed costs and variable costs based on the volumes you predicted you needed to sell.
ii. Salary – in your first month you can take a small salary but no less than 50% of what you need to earn. In the second month and beyond you must pay yourself a good full salary, that makes your lifestyle comfortable
iii. Profit must allow you to reinvest for growth and remove 20% for yourself for external Net Worth Building.
iv. Net Worth Building is anything that makes you rich but lies outside scope of this business.

10.9 Traditional Accounting Documents (TAD's)

Traditional Accounting Documents TAD's should not be seen as a TAD tiresome urges Blue Kangaroo. Most Amateur Entrepreneurs don't use them or understand them enough. But you are now a Professional Entrepreneur, aren't you?

But they can be both a TAD useful and are a TAD essential. You must learn how to use them. They are:-

i. Cash Flow
ii. Balance Sheet
iii. Profit and Loss

I will give you one single reason why these 3 Traditional Accounting Documents are so important to a successful Bounce Back and your future Wealth and Happiness.

IF YOU CANNOT USE THEM YOU CANNOT DELEGATE TO SERGEANT MAJORS AND IF YOU CANNOT DELEGATE YOU CAN NEVER GET OUT OF RUNNING YOUR BUSINESS DAY TO DAY

Look I know as Entrepreneurs with past history you have heard of these before. Previously "failed" entrepreneurs (100 surveyed) with an average of 6 years self-employed business experience cannot use them. This is how they described their knowledge of the following:-

Bouncepreneur's Ability to Use Traditional Accountancy Documents (TAD's) % Base 100				
Tool/Knowledge	Solid	Basic	Wobbly	Awful
Cash Flow Forecast	26	24	35	15
Balance Sheet	15	18	20	47
Profit and Loss	14	17	23	46

You can see it is not very good at all. Blue Kangaroo believes many, many small business owners fake their understanding – especially or balance sheets and profit and loss.

But the professional cadre largely ignore this ignorance amongst small business owners like it is not there. This makes the entrepreneur very vulnerable indeed.

Let's face it for many of us the only time we really look at them is at year end, or when we were chasing someone to give us money, or for a tender.

Good Advice from Blue Kangaroo

Free training on these tools is widely available. Just search online. To learn these three instruments will take a course lasting 4-8 hours.

One day or even half a day. It is not much time is it?

Understanding them makes you unassailable by Dingoes.

Plus these 3 documents are helpful. They really are.

You may prefer to learn them on paper before you go onto online accounts software.

Here is a brief description of each of them.

Cash Flow Statement.

A cash flow stops you unknowingly running out of cash.

Identifies potential shortfalls in cash in advance – think of the cash flow forecast as an "early warning system". This is traditionally seen as the most important reason for a cash flow forecast

It ensures the business can afford to pay suppliers and employees.

SAMPLE 6 MONTH CASHFLOW FORECAST							
NB. *For demonstration only and not reflective of a Bounce Back Cash Flow*							
	Jan	Feb	March	April	May	June	Total
Cash In							
Investment	10,000						
Sales	2,500	10,000	10,000	10,000	10,000	10,000	52,500
Total Inflow	12,500						
Cash Out							
Materials		3000	3000	3000	3000	3000	15,000
Labour	4000	4000	4000	4000	4000	4000	24,000
Marketing	500	500	500	500	500	500	3,000
Legal & Professional Services	1250						1250
Equipment	2500			2500			5000
Bouncepreneur's Salary	1000	1000	1000	1000	1000	1000	6000
Other Costs	500	500	500	500	500	500	3000
Total Outflow	9750	9000	9000	11,500	9000	9000	57,250
Net Cash Flow	2750	1000	1000	-1500	1000	1000	5250
Opening Bank Balance	0	2750	3750	4750	3250	4250	
Closing Bank Balance	2750	3750	4750	3250	4250	5250	

Balance Sheet

Your balance sheet gives an overall financial snapshot of your small business.

From a maths perspective, the two sides of the equation are

Liabilities + Owner's Equity = Assets.

The two sides of the equation must balance out.

Assets are current or fixed.

Current assets are cash or other holdings that are liquid enough to be quickly changed to cash such as money owed to you, or stock.

Fixed assets are essentials you are not planning to sell like equipment, machines, land, buildings or furniture.

An example Balance Sheet can be seen below.

Example Balance Sheet as of 31st December 2016		
Assets		
Fixed Assets	10000	
Intangible Assets	5000	
		15000

Currents Assets		
Bank	1000	
Stock	500	
Debtors	2500	
		3500
Total Assets		18500
Less Creditors Falling Due in Less Than 1 Year		
Creditors	3000	
Loan	500	
		3500
Creditors Falling Due After 1 Year		
Loan	2000	2000
		5500
Net Assets		13000
Capital and Reserves		
Issued Share Capital		2000
Reserves		11000
		13000

Profit and Loss Statement

A profit and loss statement, supposedly enables you to project sales and expenses. It typically covers a period of a year. But it becomes much more useful if it is used for shorter periods, especially quarterly.

To get net profit, you subtract total operating expenses from gross profit. (Gross profit – total operating expenses = net profit.)

Gross profit is calculated as total sales value minus the cost of products/services sold – often called Goods.

Costs of goods sold includes raw materials, stock you are holding and even owed payroll taxes.

What makes the P&L useful is the fact that as an analysis you HAVE to factor in overhead costs like utilities, insurance, repairs and professional fees into your operating expenses to ensure your net profit is accurate. Many small business actually ignore these and pay them themselves without capturing the expenses or receipts.

How many of you have lost that invoice whether it be online or down the front of your van's dashboard!

An example Profit and Loss Statement is shown below.

Example Profit & Loss Statement		
Sales		
Widgets	120000	
Total Sales		120000
Cost of Sales		
Cost of Goods Sold	40000	
Direct Labour	20000	
Total Cost of Sales		60000

Gross Profit		60000
Overheads		
Salaries	28000	
Car & Travel	3200	
Rent/Rates/Utilities/ Insurance	2500	
Telephone & Stationery	2500	
Advertising	500	
Interest	200	
Bank Charges	200	
Legal Fees	500	
Depreciation	200	
Corporation Tax	5000	
Total Overheads		42800
Profit/Loss		17200
NB: Not representative of Bouncepreneur Start-up		

10.10 Separate business and personal finances

I know that sometimes businesses have adequate money to grow, but success can make owners make careless mistakes with money.

Whatever you do, tells a stern looking Blue Kangaroo, do not blend your personal and business financials. By all means use your hard saved cash as start-up investment, do back yourself. But if you put £2,000 in get £2,000 back out.

Do not pay for business expenses from your own pocket. Likewise don't be taking your kids to the cinema with your business debit card.

Once you have a dedicated account for your business conduct all transactions through that account.

ALL transactions. Repeats Blue Kangaroo firmly.

If you do not separate your personal and venture finances, you will end up with tax problems. Then you will be doing three things:-

1. Paying tax on money you already paid tax on
2. Spending a fraught month before annual return deadlines cleaning up a mess of paperwork
3. Being very, very distressed and frankly that is just very, very unpleasant

10.11 Don't Have Partners, Loans or Equity You Just Don't Need

A very innovative man I know reached 65 at time of writing this book. He had created a very clever invention benefiting remote communities around the world. He had taken a finance for equity deal from a major investor. But he had not really needed to. Now at 65 the innovator wanted to float or sell his significant equity in the company to retire. But the equity he had given up came with small print which prevented him from making a sale of any of his equity. So none of his efforts could be transformed into cash for his retirement.

Equity is as much about staying in control as it is money.

Many of the start-up ideas I see can get going and succeed on a much smaller budgets than convention recognises.

Blue Kangaroo does not disapprove of borrowing money from banks and investors.

BUT it is not the Bouncepreneurs Way.

Start with a small venture- make it work – then use your 20% net worth income from it to fund your next venture.

10.12. Final Dingo Criticism for You to Answer

Remember I promised a final Dingo Criticism – well here it is.

Dingo Says – Bouncepreneur you don't have any clue about normal accounting

Blue Kangaroo Says – Yes I do. I confidently use 3 TAD Traditional Accounting Systems but I am not a slave to them.

You Say
_____
_____

Your Response so learn your TAD's Bouncepreneurs

10.13. Blue Kangaroo's Key Lessons

In this Chapter you have met Blue Kangaroo. He has given you plain lessons regarding your mandatory skills to protect yourself from the Dingoes and to plan effectively for a Bouncepreneur business.

He says simply HugeCorp's accounting and business planning methods serve them not you. BUT there is an element of work you must do to conform to tax and legislative requirements

Do not confuse the above as effective planning tools

He has given you a couple of very simply planning forms to keep you effective and focused

Blue Kangaroo has told you in very straightforward terms that if you don't learn the 3 key Traditional Accounting Documents or TAD's then you will always be vulnerable in your business.

Blue Kangaroo's final words of advice are to source and learn an accounting software package. Once you get that under you belt you become unassailable to the Dingoes at HugeCorp.

You know how much Blue Kangaroo hates HugeCorp!

Now Blue Kangaroo has to be going its poker night for him and he does so enjoy fleecing his local bank manager and accountant at cards. With a wave of cigar smoke Blue Kangaroo is gone.

Here comes Brown Kangaroo as ever, she is bang on time, such a capable Kangaroo Guide. Maybe that's why the other Kangaroo Guides call her Capability Brown.

CONGRATULATIONS YOU ARE NOW A BLUE BELT BOUNCEPRENEUR

11 Capability Brown Kangaroo Guide

11.1 Introduction

Brown Kangaroo or Capability Brown as her fellow Guides call her is the Guide who will make you Capable in key areas of your business venture. Now some of you, as experienced entrepreneurs will have a good handle on some of the areas Brown Kangaroo intends to cover. But very few of you will have them all nailed down perfectly.

DO NOT REPEAT PAST MISTAKES

You have come so far since losing an earlier venture, learnt so much and worked so hard.

But now we need to absolutely certain you achieve your goal – YOUR MONEY ENGINE.

So in this Chapter your Brown Kangaroo Guide will be focusing on you running your business to the point where you can step out and become the Chairperson. Specifically we are looking to highlight those reasons which might lead to business failure, even though you have established a distinct customer need and have a good product to sell.

Do bear in mind the goal here is successfully launch then get out of your business operationally by 6 months. Yes 6 months!

Your Brown Kangaroo Guide believes there are 4 BIG CHALLENGES which can prevent you moving the business from the first 30 days to a successful first 6 months.

She emphasises this is on the basis your business has definitely identified a clear customer need Plus it has proven it will sell during the 30 day BMVP phase. Brown Kangaroo Guide also assumes that many of the routine business activities you will need to complete are hard work. Especially at the beginning when it is just you. But she prefers to focus on those Challenges that really define the first 6 months of business success.

11.2. The 4 Big Challenges

Brown Kangaroo Guide tells you the 4 Big Challenges are:-

Making your product/service Discoverable by many customers - **Discoverability**

Using your limited time to best advantage – **Ruthless Attention Management**

Sloppy book keeping and accounting knowledge – **Become an Accountant**

Slipping off the Getoutable plan – **False Coaches**

Discoverability - Ruthless Attention Management - Become an Accountant - False Coaches

Before looking at the 4 Challenges Brown Kangaroo has a few words on selling. Some early readers of this book have asked why selling not one of your 4 Challenges. This is why....

WITHOUT DISCOVERABILITY THERE ARE NO SALES?

Some Bouncepreneurs have asked Brown Kangaroo why she does not say marketing. Surely you mean marketing and not just discoverability.

No we mean DISCOVERABILTY is Brown Kangaroo's response.

During your time launching your product with Green Kangaroo and the pre-testing work you did with Yellow and Orange Kangaroo, you saw that the key to your success is based on nailing the customer need.

But now your need is to Scale Up and Duplicate your business to grow. Now if you cannot get your message out to enough potential customers and be discovered then you are not going to make it.

So underpins Brown Kangaroo your absolute focus is on **DISCOVERABILTY**.

11.3. Discoverability your Biggest Success Challenge

11.3.1. Your Skills and Challenges

Brown Kangaroo Guide simply informs her students –

To be a Bouncepreneur you **HAVE** to be digitally savvy. You have to be.

Learn, learn and learn. Do not find anyone to act as your crutch – you have to understand it.

Digital software and strategy education is now widely available, cheap and sometimes free. This investment in your own skills is vital. But take education on digital strategy first. You will always be offered more and more applications to help your business to buy and learn. But remember the Tarzan rope scenario swinging from one piece of software to another without end. But although software changes all the time a good Discovery strategy will last.

Most entrepreneurs are now pretty technically savvy, certainly social media savvy. But making your product discoverable online is simply not that easy. Especially early on when resources are very limited.

A clear, affordable, manageable strategy is vital believes Brown Kangaroo.

By being confident with hosting, building a website, e-commerce, understanding SEO and even analytics you can really progress encourages Brown Kangaroo Guide.

Too many entrepreneurs try to simply outsource their digital discoverability to a website builder and do not choose to understand core details.

This is suicidal and wide open to problems.

There is a strong case to sub-contract digital activity to a 3rd party agency. This can massively reduce the Bouncepreneurs work load AND the agency can really help move your discoverability, brand quality and customer service forward.

In fact your Brown Kangaroo Guide does recommend using an agency ONCE you understand digital AND can afford an agency. But whether you use your own employees, or an agency downstream you must always:-

a. Own
b. Understand
c. Be Able to Shut Out Rogue Staff or Agencies

From your digital presence.

So as a <u>minimum</u> you must have total control of your

a. URL Ownership
b. Web space Access
c. Email account
d. Other Social Media Accounts and Names

Brown Kangaroo suggests personal Capability. She suggests that every Bouncepreneur should be able to use WordPress and be able to build a basic site.

Why?

Brown Kangaroo believes a website build is not only a marketing tool, but it is actually a great way to plan and control your business. If you can build a site which takes care of discoverability, payments, customer service and some back office operations, then you get a great feel for how the business is likely to function before it is launched. You may not actually use the site you yourself have built. But the experience is vital. Brown Kangaroo emphasises that a Bouncepreneur who can use WordPress is far less likely to be taken for a ride by a web-designer, digital agency or member of staff.

She has some thoughts for you to consider:-

- Do you have the technical skills to do what you need online?
- Can you afford to subcontract?
- Do you have the skill to control your digital subcontractor's?
- Can you get discoverability using your website/social media for free?
- Can you afford to pay for social media advertising?
- Can you use analytics?

As a Bouncepreneur you are in this business to make it Scalable, Duplicable and Getoutable remember. So if you are looking at setting up a Discoverable business you ACTUALLY need some or maybe all of the following resources and skills?

- CRM
- Campaign Tool

- Social Media Sites – the main ones AND there are always more aren't there!!!
- Social Media Feed Aggregator
- Some API Links
- Website
- SEO
- E commerce
- E Commerce to Accounts software link
- Graphic design
- Video explainer
- Channel integration mobile/voice/online
- Apps

But Brown Kangaroo emphasises SOME. You have to balance the time, scale and expense of your new venture against your product type, market and need.

Some Bouncepreneurs are simply over-committed to digital activities against their business type. Others are not committed enough. Brown Kangaroo aims to help you calibrate this level of commitment further.

11.3.2. Expert Opinion

Your Brown Kangaroo Guide is very much for the Art of the Possible, but shares her frustration that there is no consistency in terms of expert advice on digital marketing strategies for the small business owner. None!

So Bouncepreneur try to set a Discoverability strategy you are happy with and do not feel the need to justify it to anyone – except customers of course.

Some of you will really have to do more to make your Bounce Back business Discoverable versus your earlier failed venture. But other will need to do less than before. Yes less!

Here some real expert Bouncepreneurs testimony on their previous failure to get Discoverability right.

Brown Kangaroo Guide does not expect you to take her word for it. Ever capable she has real world testimony from Bouncepreneurs at their White Kangaroo stage to remind you what the pitfalls can be.

"I spent all my spare cash on online social media advertising –absolute waste of time. Mine was a local city market. But my advertising was national. Before I really understood how the advertising worked I'd blown my budget."

"Trouble was the social media target categories were so general I couldn't get near the profile of the customers I was really after."

"Although I am over 50 I am no IT slouch. Far from it. But I was spending 7 hours of my working day promoting the business, writing blogs and trying to hook various systems together. But the harder I worked the more complex and expensive everything got. I still had my day job to do making our product. Very soon I was snappy, broke and exhausted."

"The only people reading my promotions were marketing people, the more I worked on marketing my own service the more crap I got pouring in from software, vendors and consultants. I only wanted to find some customers, but I just couldn't seem to do that!"

11.3.3. Discoverability can Kill Your Venture

Brown Kangaroo Guide becomes very serious now.

Brown Kangaroo and all the other Kangaroo Guides share the same belief that Discoverability is now the biggest challenge facing the Bouncepreneur and any start-up in fact. Even assuming they have tested and proven customer need for their idea.

Discoverability is making your offering seen by prospective customers, not great surprise there. But Bouncepreneurs have told us that getting noticed was enormously challenging.

Failure to be discoverable is killing many ventures start-ups AND mature businesses. Do not be one of the small businesses throwing money, they don't have, at online advertising. Especially advertising that isn't going to work for them.

11.3.4. Fear of No Discoverability

Research has shown that Bouncepreneurs do not suffer Fear of Failure across their business like a first time start up would. But they do have real fear about specific aspects of their business.

It does not surprise Brown Kangaroo that so many Bouncepreneurs are really frightened of making their business discoverable.

She recommends that you be FAR more selective and confident when listening to the vast quantities and material and advice out there in La La Land in making your business Discoverable. Conflicting advice will otherwise drive yourself crazy with worry, overwork or spending on channels that will bear no fruit.

Seeing a clear strategy, even for someone as capable as Brown Kangaroo Guide Discoverability is a challenge. She believes that this is because the vast majority of advice is not written for the typical start up entrepreneur. But for more specialist individuals or vendor software suppliers, such as:-

- Start-ups based on online business services such as software and publishing
- Individuals with strong online or software coding experience
- Software for the start-up to buy
- Software for the start-up to buy which mandates the purchase of further software
- Large advertising giants whose methods can work for HugeCorp with huge budgets but really do not work for limited cash start ups
- Start-ups whose products fit the geographical/business type categories of social media advertising platforms
- Software which you must buy with expensive training to use properly

Brown Kangaroo Guide strongly recommends education as the key to beating the Fear of Discoverability.

11.3.5. Not All Discovery Comes From Proactive Online Marketing

Brown Kangaroo Guide has some useful ways for you to think about Discoverability.

a. Your business will only grow offline and online if you can get the message to spread. Your online presence may just be about helping people to find you and not to promote.

b. Technology **is** going to be the backbone of your business whether you write software applications or have a chain of coffee shops

c. If you are spending **all** your time on discovery in your first six months you do not have enough pull in terms of customer need for your product

d. Your growth should be built on getting you message to spread with a Happy Customers – Come Back Regularly – Tell Their Friends – More Customers mentality.

11.3.6. What You Must Do

Although not all discovery comes from proactive online marketing, you will always need:-

- A professional online presence
- A means for people to learn about your story
- A means to allow your story to spread
- A manageable level of work
- An affordable level of work

11.3.7. Brown Kangaroo's Top 10 Tips on Discoverability and Digital Marketing

- Piggy backing well known distribution channels is cheap and quick
- You can be both <u>discovered</u> and sell things on Amazon
- You can be both <u>discovered</u> and sell things on eBay or Schpock
- Even though you can sell things from your site via e-commerce, if you are not discoverable this does not matter
- By making a full time job of social media marketing/website other elements may fail
- You may not get a return on bought advertising your products on social media
- SEO is getting easier thanks to businesses like Yoast

- Building websites is also getting easier and template driven
- Websites building tools with built in e-commerce are very greedy, always research what you will pay before you start using an app. Even if it is on free trial (your time is not free!)

11.3.8. Appropriate Digital Channel for Discoverability

But there are still people around the world who make businesses work without spending 90% of their time online AND it is important to say this. But some Bouncepreneurs are purely online business models selling software and digital training for example.

The small coffee shop chain needs to make customers feel loved at each of their locations. The engineering company needs to equip their distribution network with maximum technical and demonstration support and the software company selling to SME's needs super SEO to breakthrough competition and reach their intended market.

But you must remember that not all businesses are based on online models. So their Discoverability needs are going to be different.

<u>Hospitality is a good example of course.</u>

The very successful Brunning and Price gastro pub chain extending throughout the UK had a competent by very small web presence. But word of mouth spread because of the chain's great interiors and nice atmospheres. But managers and servers who clearly were a cut above the normal pub leadership adding to the feeling of quality. This is what made this chain successful. – This led to word of mouth based growth without a doubt.

<u>Engineering is another</u>

Bladon Jets make an electricity generator that can power villages without the need for mains electricity. A boon for isolated communities in many countries. Especially useful where power is needed to power cellular networks.

The use of a very small jet engine with much lower running and maintenance costs than a typical diesel generator makes this a really interesting product. By partnering with local distributors who already know the market this great technology will realise it's potential.

Of course it needs to be demonstrable online. But discoverability to distributors was best achieved by traditional proactive sales contact. Bladon would not be able to reach civic leaders in isolated communities, but local distributors were already servicing their needs.

There is in fact a Spectrum of Discoverability

The Spectrum of Discoverability		
Coffee Shop Chain	**Engineering Business**	**Software Vendor**
Serving Local City or Town Catchments (Chain)	Selling Specialist Higher Value or B2B Products Online	Selling Digital Service Online
You will need a friendly, local-feel and compact online presence replicated as your chain builds	You will need to demonstrate your product and support your distribution channels	You will be fighting for top position on the search engines and SEO will be critical to your success
Discoverability achieved by – High footfall physical location – bring a friend campaign – loyalty campaigns – local community events – local micro sponsorship	Discoverability achieved by – Specialist selling based on identifying local distributors i.e. indirect sales. Modest promotional website with strong product demonstration	Discoverability achieved by – Hard core SEO success in competitive space. Analytics of advertising and online placement in Google AdWords, PPC for example

With these examples Brown Kangaroo makes the point that not every business needs the same OR in fact the same coverage. But not for the founder to spend 24/7 online trying to crack open online sales which there are different opportunities to achieve discoverability.

11.4 Ruthless Attention Management

11.4.1. What is it?

It is time for a different approach to managing your time. Brown Kangaroo wants to help you become more capable. She says you should give up trying time management. It just leads to daily feelings of failure and frustration. Instead think about

RUTHLESS ATTENTION MANAGEMENT

Firmly Brown Kangaroo states –

A. You are going to decide to be ruthless in what you allow your attention to dwell on

B. And you are going to mindfully manage your attention.

Why?

In recent years managing your time has become very difficult indeed. In fact it has become incredibly stressful. Distractions come from every corner, every device demanding attention and the volume of information coming towards us is increasingly unpleasant.

Yes UNPLEASANT.

It does not seem to matter how much time you have, how far you extend your day, managing time is such a challenge. You are under attack from information overload 24 hours a day.

Many failed entrepreneurs report that no matter how hard they tried getting control of "time" was a huge challenge. "*I spent too long working on the wrong things*" is such a common from "Failed" Entrepreneurs.

Keeping your focus, maintaining a healthy focus on your own goals – not anyone else's! Is the key skill needed to ensure our own success in our commercial ventures and life outside work?

By focusing on our own "Positive" Goals we enter the state of progression which builds over time. But if we allow our focus to dwell on "negative" attention – by that Brown Kangaroo means not our own goals will build a downward spiral of failure which easily deteriorates into a depressive state.

Some people describe this as vibration. But it must be true that we have a much higher chance to achieve our own wants and desires if we focus on them and exclude things we do not want. She suggests that you:-

Watch Yourself Mindfully - Be mindful of your attention. Study and watch yourself on where and how you are directing your attention. If you let it your attention roam free, it will run wild and go in any direction it chooses – often haphazardly.

Be Very Ruthless - We have started a new venture to become successful. When we are making progress against our own plans we feel really good and fulfilled. The works that feels best is when we are moving forward, doing what we planned. Ruthlessly hold to your plan.

Don't Play the Defensive Game - We STILL spend too much time playing the defensive game. Responding to other people's contact, social media, 24/7 news feed and many, many attempts to sell things to our business we do not need. Your time is for your business goals. Just yours.

Remember Your Attention is a Finite Resource - You must decide to be VERY RUTHLESS about what you spend your Attention on as it is a finite resource. Plus you are not going to be working within this venture in six months.

Have a Default Statement for Saying No - You have to keep your commitments tight. If you do not, you will water down your focus on your own goals.

So Brown Kangaroo Guides you to develop a stock phrase or way to say no. Plan a way of saying no

- In person
- In social media
- On the phone
- In email

Do not Offer Your Advice, Time or Resources for Free – Do not squander any of these limited resources. Respect their value yourself. If you do not, no-one else will.

Don't Respond to Guilt - Finally, some people around you will use guilt as a weapon when you say no. Do not allow yourself to feel guilty for saying no. You have experienced business failure once – do not allow the Time Bandits to do it twice.

Consider Buying a Dumb Phone – This may be a bit extreme for some of you. But at time of writing my smartphone failed. Because I know there is a new version of it coming out in a couple of months, I decided to use an old phone for a while. This old phone has no internet connection, just texts, calls and a camera. Since using it my productivity soared.

You can still tap into emails and social media using other devices, but give controlled attention.

Then I read Nokia are reintroducing a revamped version of a phone they originally sold in the noughties – a dumbphone. Sales of this type of phone are apparently climbing steadily, especially in major financial centres like London. Nokia seem to have realised that many people want to get their lives back from the bombardment of meaningless information in order to focus on their own objectives and goals.

Watch Out for Machine Gun Distractions - Once your attention is distracted a single time, one tends to find it is not a single shot, but a machine gun of negative Time Bandits.

So once you see that first attention stealer, do EVERYTHINGT to stop it dead as soon as possible and prevent the machine gun filling your attention with holes.

Have a "default" positive to quickly switch your attention to. Since negative thoughts can quickly occupy our mind, Brown Kangaroo suggests you find ways to get out quickly. To do so, you need a "default" positive to which you can quickly switch your attention.

One thing you can use as default positive is inspiring and motivating quotes. When you start paying attention to negative thoughts, quickly switch your attention to the inspiring quotes to get yourself back on track.

Concentration Music - If you play the theme to Rocky or something more contemporary (what can I say I love Rocky and I am middle aged!) to help you in the gym or running you will understand the motivational effects of music.

One of the great aids Brown Kangaroo Guide recommends for improving attention span and concentration is Solfeggio music. Check them out for yourself on YouTube. There are many variations on the ideas of using music to help you concentrate.

But these tend to be chants, specific frequency music and even bells. They originate from wide and varied religious and non-religious sources. But they are enormously useful aids to focus attention.

Know When to Take a Break - Brown Kangaroo is very capable and knows when she needs to take a break. Her passion is renovating classic cars. She describes it a Getting Return on Investment (ROI) from Your Attention.

Sometimes one can spend hours trying to complete a task. You expect it to take an hour but three hours later the end is not in sight. The ROI is poor. You have to know when to stop and give it another try later. Pouring more and more energy in will frustrate you, produce diminishing payback and become demotivating.

Stop – go on to something else. Think! Your attention is valuable. The most valuable thing you have in fact.

Not All Your Work Has to be at a Desk or Workbench - Why not do a daily planning review while you exercise. I often run a Planning Review through my head as I train in the swimming pool!

As a Bouncepreneur you will know your plan intimately. It will be on your mind like a tattoo. So take time daily to review it and the main goals you are working towards. But do not do this at a desk. Review your plan while swimming in the pool (I do) or jogging or walking the dog. I find this gives me the best ideas and clarity. I can focus whilst swimming on the plan, challenges and potential solutions.

Delegation and Taking on Other People's Attention - As your business grows and you delegate using your clear job descriptions, you may find your own attentions are tied up doing your employee's work. Avoid this at all costs advices Brown Kangaroo.

The stupidest phrase of all time is

"If you want something doing right you have to do it yourself!"

Brown Kangaroo remembers a story she was once told of an expanding entrepreneur hiring an office manager to keep the office running smoothly in terms of cleaning, utilities, repairs and so on. A few weeks after starting there was a need to clean a water dispenser. It was part of the office manager's responsibilities the entrepreneur believed. But the manager did not want to clean it himself. It was a bit of a messy task, but something the small business owner would not have thought twice about doing it herself in the past.

One summer evening she found herself in the office late cleaning this water dispenser. She was angry because she was doing this job after her own working day and the office manager danced out of the office to a barbeque. She was paying for this task to receive the attention of her office manager, yet I was doing the job herself.

The following day she spoke to the employee he said aggressively "I didn't take this job to be a skivvy!"

The entrepreneur then went away thinking that maybe it was a cleaning job and beneath his job grade after all.

But then I realised as a company of just 30 staff, this was his responsibility. That sort of office management role WAS in his job description and how he solved the problem was his concern.

So as your business follows the Bouncepreneurs model and you appoint your Sergeant Major Kangaroos, make very sure they take Attention away from you. Do not allow your attention to be drained into your staff's responsibilities.

<u>Thinking Time & Time Off</u> - Your success will require more than mindless hard work. You will hit unexpected barriers. You will certainly have to find ways of moving forward without money.

To do this you are going to need creative problem solving. This type of process only comes when you are relaxed and can think straight. By taking yourself out of the business process and social media distractions, you can get past barriers and come up with new ideas to move forward.

Often the best ideas come along at the strangest times. Walking the dog, pushing the kids on the swings, in a dream, watching a movie, on a beach in Spain.

Time off is essential to maintain creative thought energy

11.4. Becoming an Accountant

Brown Kangaroo suggests this is the best plan for Bouncepreneurs. Simply become a better accountant than your accountant. This gives you huge advantages in terms of:-

- Profitability
- Tax liability
- Self confidence
- Reduced accounting bills

Get or make a calendar - showing the key tax return, VAT or other accounting requirements in your country. Then mark in your own annual return dates, VAT periods, and so on. Be humble, even if you have run a business for 20 years in the past, make sure you get these right.

Watch the budget - Every year – sometimes more often your government minister will announce changes to tax and tax regulations in your country. Make sure you watch this and read a good review in the followings days. It is worth buying and keeping a newspaper in the days after any budget.

Leaving until last minute - This is definitely the most common issue. Leave alone, leave alone, leave alone PANIC! Brown Kangaroo advises do a little as your go along every day. Set any afternoon aside every week purely for accounting.

Using software – Once you understand the Traditional Accounting Documents or TAD's go onto electronic software. But Brown Kangaroo Guide does suggest you might want to learn your craft on paper first. But there are advantages in using software BUT ONLY IF YOU UNDERSTAND IT. Brown Kangaroo advises understanding is more important than speed early on.

Also buy software which suits the size of your business. Buying software which is too big for your business can cause huge problems so go small to start with. Also you may not have to buy accounting software at all. New banking apps are now emerging which have built in accounting software within your online app. The big accounting software companies will not like this, but their cash cow is about to be seriously disrupted. So buy wisely.

Having a separate bank account – Although a separate bank account will cost you. Working off a single personal account can be difficult especially when it comes to your tax return. However if you are a sole trader, there is no reason suggests Brown Kangaroo why you should not have two personal bank accounts with different banks. This saves you bank charges in your early days. If you mix your business and personal finances, your will make life very difficult and actually probably lose tax deductible items along the way.

Not filing bank statements in order - It sounds simple, but you'd be amazed how many people don't do it. What happens? You give your statements to your accountant at year-end and they phone back later to tell you a statement is missing. This means you've just paid your accountant (who probably charges by the hour), to organise your bank statements, when you could have saved money by doing it yourself.

Organised filing - Be like Brown Kangaroo Capable! Be proud of your filing system and organisation. File in date order. Split invoices into paid and not paid purchase invoices.

Have a distinct place and files for your business - Ideally a dedicated office if you work at home – even if it is a Harry Potter office under the stairs. There are some great ideas for small offices on Pinterest.

Be fastidious in retaining purchase receipts as you go - On your accounting afternoon gather all your loose receipts from your car, van dash board, wallet, gym bag. purse, attache case or tool bench. Make sure you scoop them all up weekly. Be fastidious. Trying to back track and work out your year's business costs is horrible. You will also pay more tax than you should do. Keep a close record of every penny your business spends emphasises Brown Kangaroo.

11.6. False Coaches

Once your business starts to fire and sales start to flow, be sure the Dingoes will come out of every corner. Often time the same people who refused or called in your loan ironically. The support agencies will start calling you.

Brown Kangaroo tells you do not be seduced by them. They have nothing to offer you.

You have a solid plan based on Scale Up, Duplication and Getoutability. SUDGO

It is a process you can start small and repeat so you end up owning multiple businesses.

You do not need alternative business models urges Brown Kangaroo.

If anyone approaches you to discuss selling or investing in your business before you reach you six month goal, give them the following challenge. This was great advice given to me by a senior in Coutts Bank

"Ask your potential investor or buyer to write down a number on a cheque or even piece of paper as their bid for your company and bring it with them. If they cannot do that, they are not senior or serious enough and are just wasting your time."

Remember most of the coaching you will hear will emanate from three main sources:-

- Hugecorp who operate on an entirely different model from you
- Agencies who exist for political not commercial masters
- People who want to sell you their way of doing things

But do remember one key fact that false coaches will never acknowledge and it is this:-

IF YOU HAVE SALES EVERYTHING ELSE IS JUST SOLID WORK

Speaking to real life Bouncepreneurs I always hear a very consistent story. It will come as no surprise to you that your fellow Bouncepreneurs all believed lack of sales to be the main cause of their original venture's failure.

Failed ventures where the structure and management of the business was generally pretty solid and failed normally see the lack of sales as the key problem.

IF SALES ARE GOOD BUSINESS IS STRAIGHTFORWARD

Now I hear some say "Yes but how long will the business be solid is there are underlying problems being propped up by good sales."

Well Brown Kangaroo would argue there are many, many very large companies who do many things badly, but are thriving.

The fact of the matter is this, if a business has strong revenue flow, the rest of it is just WORK.

Making the product, delivering the service, running the office, saying thank you to customers, researching customer feedback, accounts, recruitment and book-keeping, recruitment

It is all just work. Albeit work that should be done professionally, diligently and with enthusiasm.

YOU ONLY GET PROBLEMS WHEN REVENUE IS NOT THERE

So long as you have sales revenue coming in and your business model is sound in terms of reasonable longevity and profitability, then you can:-

- Pay your suppliers
- Pay your staff
- Order that machine
- Get that salon fit out
- Refurbish that old bar
- Buy the CRM software

11.7. Brown Kangaroo's Key Lessons

Brown Kangaroo smiles knowingly and shakes your hand warmly. She knows you have taken her four key lessons on board.

Discoverability – Balance getting found online with appropriate workload

Ruthless Attention Management – know what is worthy use of your limited time

Become an Accountant – Be a better accountant than your accountant

False Coaches – you do not need approval, carve your own destiny

Before going the Capability Brown says we are finished a few minutes early, but Black Kangaroo will be along shortly. You'll enjoy meeting him (and his wife) most of all she promises. Then with a confident smile that tells you she thinks you are going to become both rich and happy, she bounces off down the street. Capability Brown is finishing early, because she is more than on top of her work.

CONGRATULATIONS YOU ARE NOW A BROWN BELT BOUNCEPRENEUR

12 Black Belt Bouncepreneur

12.1. Introduction

Black Kangaroo Guide meets you in his favourite coffee bar. Immediately you can see a casually dressed, relaxed and happy person. He exudes confidence.

He is accompanied by his partner. She is equally calm and relaxed. Like Black Kangaroo Guide she has the blackest, fantastic hair. It is no surprise to hear she too is a Black Belt Bouncepreneur. The couple work in totally different businesses but have recovered from business failure in a similar way.

Black Kangaroo Guide gets a warm kiss on the cheek and a hand on his shoulder as she leaves us alone, while she takes a meeting or her own down the street.

Now Black Kangaroo has the aura of wealth. He has been a Guide to many Bouncepreneurs who have followed the Bounce Back Pathway. His main role is to help you cement the success of your new venture so that it gives you the best possible yield towards long term success and happiness.

As a Black Kangaroo you have reached the highest level of success as a Bouncepreneur. You have established a successful business.

- That pays you a great salary
- Where you take out 20% of the profits in addition to your salary
- That you have no operational management work
- And you have a strong executive management team and Managing Director
- Your role is that of Chairperson

You have established wealth and happiness. But Black Kangaroo Guide speaks to you peer to peer about NEVER falling backwards again.

"Business is Snake and Ladders"

His advice shows you how to move even further forward in building success and happiness.

Your Black Kangaroo Guide sits next to you, orders your favourite coffee. There is an understanding between you of mutual respect, past hard times and a journey of recovery that only those who have walked it fully understand.

The thing about Black Kangaroos is that they often live in trees. They are great climbers and this one is going to show you how to climb further than the success of your first Bounce Back business.

In this Chapter Black Kangaroo Guide will discuss with you 10 Ideas for Sustained Success. These Ideas Cover:-

1. Being strong with Your Executive Team
2. Remembering you Are the Entrepreneur
3. Becoming a Serial Entrepreneur
4. Investing Outside of Your Businesses
5. Taking Your Full Share
6. Remembering a Dingo Never Changes
7. Enjoy Your Wealth
8. Take Rest and Revival Time
9. Helping Other Bounce Back
10. Broken Man or Broken Woman

12.2. Being Strong with Your Executive Team

You will remember that the Bounce Back Pathway suggests you appoint a series of strong, order following Sergeant-Majors for each of the key areas of your business. As you appoint them in turn you step out of that area of operational management. This process culminates with the appointment of a Managing Director to lead your business plan forward.

You will own the business and be the Executive Chairman too.

The definition of an Executive Chairman varies tremendously in HugeCorp land. You and Black Kangaroo Guide laugh together knowing instinctively it will not serve you well to copy models from big banks, IT giants or parastatals. The Bouncepreneur Executive Chairman role can be defined as:-

- You are the Boss of the Managing Director
- You are a NOT operationally active
- You have a dashboard of reports which you define that the MD is responsible for giving to you
- You will judge the performance of the MD and the Executive Team on these reports
- The reports will be your guide to the success of the business
- Quarterly you will deliberately and disruptively investigate the business performance first hand
- You retain responsibility for overseas expansion, quarterly budget approval, product line expansion and Sergeant Major Executive Team and Managing Director appointments and Rewards

Professional Distance

It is essential to maintain a Professional Distance from your Executive Team. For the business to thrive you must see your team realise the growth you know the business has potential for. Therefore, emphasises Black Kangaroo Guide your leadership team must be given fair objectives AND the knowledge they MUST deliver.

No leadership team in a Bouncepreneur venture should ever feel that non-delivery is acceptable.

But reminds Black Kangaroo you must function in the "world of the possible."

Achievable Goals – Exacting Performance Monitoring – Great Reward – Intolerance of Failure

As the owner of the business you need to ensure your leadership team are motivated, successful and happy.

Rather than being bitter, cynical and twisted why not be open, honest and sincere with the leadership team.

You also need to ensure that you have succession planning in case a team members leaves AND protect yourself from the MD creating a me-too of your business without you!

You definitely need some form of golden hand cuffs on your leadership team to prevent creating a me-too competitor. But the best way of retaining your key people is a share ownership plan. Why not make your key lieutenants business owners too. But do ensure you do not dilute your ownership to the point where you lose control.

One of the exit options you can have to cash out on your business is to offer ownership to your leadership Kangaroo Sergeant Majors in the form of a Management Buyout.

There are many other permutations to consider, but the three key aspects are:-

- Ensure you have legal protection
- Being open and fair is always the best way
- Your senior staff may offer the best possible exit route for you to cash in

Dealing with and Recruiting People

When you are expanding your business, make sure you employ the best people you possibly can. Do not appoint on anything but merit.

Many entrepreneurs blame their business failure on poor recruitment. Make sticking to a plan a key virtue in your business.

Develop a culture based on key mission and key values. Do this from day one.

Black Kangaroo tells you – you will make the odd wrong appointment. Try not to, but once you realise you have got it wrong be ruthless. It is not your job to mentor your leaders, no to provide a shoulder to cry on.

But he says as he leans forward, with a very serious look in his eyes. If you appoint the wrong Sergeant-Major in your first six months, this can be a business-killer. Be prepared to be enormously ruthless at this key stage. Your appointment should be made on this person being able to run with every aspect of your job description. If you find majors flaws in the person's skills, attitude or performance GET THEM OUT. If you do not achieve the full Bounce Back within 6 months, but it takes 9 months or a year due to selecting the wrong leaders this is acceptable. It is better to build a solid foundation over 9 months than a shaky one in 6!

Good Ideas for Your People

- You will reward your leadership team well
- You will make them feel valued.
- Make them feel forward momentum

- Promote from within
- Invest in training – people will love you for it

Other Thoughts on Your Managing Director

When appointing your MD remember the following points

- A managing director does not have to earn a million a year.
- They could be part time and earn a modest wage
- They are there to ensure you plan is overseen and not to take the business off in other directions.
- His or her core job is to ensure the objectives set down in the job descriptions of your other directors are delivered and reporting is consistent with your plan. They have a job description too!
- Just because you start a business in a specific country does not mean the MD of that country should automatically be made the MD of your second country market.
- Just like any other employee the MD has to deliver the reports to you – the business owner and to be accountable for results.

12.3. Remember <u>you</u> are the Entrepreneur

Black Kangaroo Guide sits back, slowly stirring his Americano coffee. He looks at you closely and reminds you that the Bouncepreneur Bounce Back Pathway is very unconventional. You know this well by now.

He prepares you for some of the most unconventional advice of all.

- There is no such thing as completely passive income
- You must retain personal control of product innovation
- Let operational people do what you pay them for - to stick to your plan
- Give them scope to improve things but leave major innovations to yourself
- Make the mission of the business to follow your plan and grow your model through duplication
- Do not expect innovation from your team
- You be the innovator – that is your job
- Do not interlink your businesses so that in the event of failure one will drag another under
- When your product has run its course or lifespan be prepared to cull it.

12.4. Becoming a Serial Entrepreneur

You will recall from earlier Chapters that the Bouncepreneur Bounce Back Pathway advocates becoming a Serial Entrepreneur. It advocates once your first Bounce Back business is running and generating profit, you use your profits to set up another business.

Black Kangaroo Guide asks the question

"Why does the Bounce Back Pathway push becoming a serial Entrepreneur so strongly?"

You may answer along these lines

- Products and services have increasingly short life spans
- Political change can kill a product overnight
- You can have a second product in the same market
- You must never be in a situation where the downturn of a single product or business means poverty or loss to you personally
- There is a lot of opportunity out there!

But Black Kangaroo Guide suggests that you might like to add a few reasons of your own. After all you are no longer the student. You have built up a successful Bounce Back. So what do you see the advantages of being a Serial Entrepreneur over being dependent on a single product or service?

<u>Your Reasons for Becoming a Serial Bouncepreneur</u>

Ultimately, shares your Black Kangaroo Guide, the Black Belt Entrepreneur has achieved financial and personal success, so becoming a serial entrepreneur is simply an insurance policy and risk spread.

12.5. Investing Outside of Your Business

In the same way Black Kangaroo Guide suggests that you should have serial businesses, he also encourages you to invest profits outside of the business.

<u>Invest in things you understand</u>

Apps for stock market trading are advertised on the shirts of major sports stars. Throw in a few thousand bucks and test the market. That is the message Black Kangaroo, you and me may have already heard. But I do not understand the app. I do not understand the stock market very well. So do not invest.

The message is simple. Do not invest in anything you do not understand. Simply don't – emphasises Black Kangaroo Guide.

He himself either does not invest OR if he feels there is some potential he will educate himself first and then make informed investments.

<u>Do not Hand over Control of Your Investments</u>

Handing over control of your investments to a broker or agent is the same as investing in things you do not understand. Never invest in financial instruments you do not understand. Never!

You worked hard for your money – do not give it away suggests Black Kangaroo as he bites into a small bar of exquisite chocolate that is his favourite treat of the week. Spanish chocolate is his preferred option. Unconventional but better than Swiss, Belgian or Dutch he tells me, knowing the fearsome opposition that view will receive from Brussels, Amsterdam and Geneva.

<u>Start Small</u>

Property is commonly seen as a safe investment bet. Black Kangaroo Guide does not give investment advice. But renovating and reselling a house to achieve a profit is a straightforward way of expanding your wealth for sure.

Starting with a small house or apartment makes a lot of sense. Black Kangaroo Guide owns several properties. But he has also invested in garages. Just garages that he makes a solid rental income from. He also invests in precious metals and shipping containers.

<u>Give Back by Helping Fellow Bouncepreneurs</u>

He has become a source of finance to several Bouncepreneurs who he helped get restarted. This was risky he admits, but it was a way to give back that I would suggest all Black Belt Bouncepreneurs consider.

12.6. Taking your Full Share

One of the tendencies of Bouncepreneurs that have established a business is to reduce what they take out of the business if it does not achieve planned results.

Black Kangaroo Guide rolls his eyes and shakes his head, creating quite a draft from his long ears.

Never reduce your salary or profits from a business you have set up. If the business has an effective plan for growth and expansion make sure it sticks.

Take your share first. Always. If it gets to the point where the business survival depends on it retaining your salary or profits it is in deep trouble emphasises Black Kangaroo.

If you have to get involved in operations to save it your team has failed, market conditions may have changed. But never pay your executive team before yourself. They control the business and they must find the savings if the business have not achieved target.

Protect your wealth and be very ruthless in taking your full share. If the business falls behind, make it very clear to the leadership that you are not a charitable person prepared to plug holes with your own money.

Never, never stay with a failing business model advises Black Kangaroo. Because that is how we both her in the first place he states in a sombre mood.

12.7. Remember a Dingo Never Changes

One thing you can be very sure of says Black Kangaroo Guide. You know what he is going to say before he even has to say it.

You know that now you are making money and lots of it, the Dingoes will return. Just like when your business failed the Dingoes will sniff a profit and return.

Like an old boomerang here they come, says Black Kangaroo – a bad memory of his Grief quickly crosses he mind, but he shakes it away quickly.

This time they will be looking to invest in you. Imagine that laughs Black Kangaroo darkly. Their cohorts will be telling you that you need investors and support to ramp up scale.

The Dingoes are back!

But you must not let them distract you says Black Kangaroo, gripping your arm with very serious intent. Do not let the Dingoes in.

<u>Dingoes Kill Kangaroos!</u>

You are in control of your own destiny.

Your business idea has worked. You can create your own new venture capital now. You do not need investors. The last thing you need is investors distracting you from your main goal which is Ramping Up not a beauty parade for money you no longer need.

You can now capitalise the working capital needs of second, third and multiple businesses without external investment. As a Professional Entrepreneur you will need to have several businesses. You have made the first one all about topping up your personal wealth.

Make the next business you roll even better, faster and more successful.

Remember what we said about Approval. As a Professional Entrepreneur you don't need it. You don't need the advice of stranger- investors on your customers or your processes.

If you have done your homework diligently you simply do not need it.

12.8. Enjoy Your Wealth

Black Kangaroo Guide takes out his wallet and shows me the first of four photographs.

<u>Enjoy What YOU enjoy</u>

In the first photograph there is a Triumph TR8 two seater convertible sports car. Apparently made way back in 1980. He is shown posing on the front next to a mountain lake. Proudly he tell me it is British Racing Green and has an original 3.5 litre engine.

Black Kangaroo bought this car because I really loves the design. To him this car was more attractive than a Ferrari or a Maserati.

Now apparently Black Kangaroo also has a very modern, fuel efficient, serious executive car, which he runs tax efficiently through his business. It is very modern yet soul-less he confides. But the upsides are the comfort on long trips, the great sound system and he likes to feel safe.

He tells me to remember Black Belt Entrepreneurs have made it! We must enjoy what WE enjoy. When he achieved a key financial milestone he decided to treat himself. He shared with me that many told him to buy a huge car, ostentatious to show off my wealth. But he did not feel the need to parade his success to gain approval. But he did want to enjoy his wealth AND have some fun.

So he bought a great executive car, for a substantial discount as it was 2 years old but like new.

But he also bought the Triumph TR8.

The TR8 cost a modest sum. It is not the most reliable of cars, he admitted, never was. Many people simply do not like them – he laughed out loud!

But Black Kangaroo loves it.

He worked with a specialist (who is now a trusted friend) to bring the car up to great condition. Now both he and his Black Belt Bouncepreneur wife enjoy taking the car up into the mountains with the roof down. It is escapism.

His Triumph is a classic car. Its value is growing – not falling and although it does cost more to service and maintain than a modern car it is his great treat.

His treat. For his success. His passion.

If you offered Black Kangaroo Guide a new Maserati, Porsche or Ferrari as a swap for his TR8 he would say no.

12.9. Take Rest and Revival Time

Now Black Kangaroo shows me a second photograph

This photograph shows him on the edge of a swimming pool sitting quietly with his wife, sipping a beer and enjoying the sunshine.

Black Kangaroo then explains that he used some of his profits to buy a nice villa. The villa is part of a nice community of people from many countries. When I am not using it we get a great rental income from it. Here he gets away from it all with his family. He rests, swims, plays tennis, enjoys warm winters and recharges.

Without a rested fresh mind there is no innovations I tell Black Kangaroo and he agrees and adds, with a fresh mind one sees light instead of dark.

Taking breaks is important.

Black Kangaroo makes his villa available to friends and family to enjoy. He returns very regularly and is looked after well by the locals.

Everyone needs a bolt hole to rest and revive.

12.10 Helping Others to Bounce Back

<u>Share Your Testimony</u>

Testimony is one of the best ways to help others Bounce Back Black Kangaroo Guide tells me. He grips my arm tightly and looks me directly in the eyes with a very steely gaze.

"You must never shirk from giving honest testimony of your failed business and challenges in making a recovery"

He emphasises the need for Bouncepreneurs to change opinions about business failure. It is his belief that Black Belt Entrepreneurs have a responsibility not just to help others Bounce Back but to change society.

<u>4 Ways to Help the Bouncepreneur Movement</u>

Black Kangaroo suggests to me 4 ways that I can help the Bouncepreneur Movement. I can tell he really believes what he is saying.

1st WAY **Help** others whose businesses have failed

2nd WAY **Jostle** the Establishment to do more for Entrepreneurs whose ventures have failed

3rd WAY **Buy from** organisations that support ethical business failure and Bounce Back

4th WAY **Reject** the idea that first time start-ups and Bouncepreneurs are the same

<u>Mentoring Bouncepreneurs</u>

Black Kangaroo Guide then shows me a picture of himself and a woman. He had his arm around this woman. The woman had no relaxation in her face, she was clearly over-weight and looked like he was carrying the weight of the world on her shoulders.

I enquired about the identity of the woman.

That is Katrin he told me. This is when I first met her. Three months before she had lost her haberdashery business. After ten years she **had** to close it all down. She was distraught. She was a Broken Woman.

He had mentored Katrin to a full Bounce Back.

Helping other "Failed Entrepreneurs" back to wealth and happiness is such a huge reward for me, he confided. Sometimes I invest capital into them to get going again. But I find it is the shared experience they really value.

12.11 Remember You Are a Broken Man or Broken Woman

Black Kangaroo Guide shows his final picture. It was a big shock.

At first I did not know who it was. It was a picture of himself.

But he looked very, very different to the suave relaxed Kangaroo of today.

In the photograph there was a Kangaroo who looked tired, broke, and agitated. The sleek black fur of today was grey and patchy. His right arm was in a sling – obviously injured. His large ears drooped down like they themselves had no fight left.

On the bottom of the photograph, in his own writing were the words in large fluorescent violet marker pen

"Broken Man."

I enquired why he kept the photograph of himself in such a wretched condition.

He then informed me this keepsake was as a reminder.

I told him I could understand why he would keep a picture to remind him of being broke and losing his business. To make sure it never happened again.

He informed me this was **not** the reason why he kept the photograph.

There was another reason which he shared with me.

Someone I loved very much told me I was a Broken Man (well Broken Kangaroo actually he smiled). This was the lowest point, worse than losing my business.

The photograph reminded him ALWAYS to back himself, to trust himself, even in the darkest days,

<u>"Even one that day the smallest glimmer of entrepreneurial spark was still alive in me ," he said.</u>

One day I said to myself *"Lift Your Head Entrepreneur – It's not over yet!"*

Then Black Kangaroo Guide took my hand and shook it warmly

CONGRATULATIONS YOU TOO ARE NOW A BLACK BELT BOUNCEPRENEUR

At that moment his wife came back to the coffee shop and Black Kangaroo called across to her

Hey Katrin its Friday Night and we are going out for a serious celebration!

Final Words

I really hope you found this book useful.

I hope your life becomes better as a result of reading it.

Always be proud of being a Bouncepreneur. Whether you are White Belt or a Black Belt.

It takes guts to Bounce Back.

Be Proud!

Best Wishes

Acknowledgements

Doctor Gabriella Cacciotti - Postdoctoral Researcher at Aalto University, Helsinki

Professor Deniz Ucbasaran – Warwick Business School

Professor Harry Hummels Maastricht University

Professor Jonathan Levie – Hunter Centre Strathclyde Business School

Professor Mark Hart - Aston Business School

Doctor Katia Pina – Southampton Business School

Professor Orla Byrne – Michael Smurfitt Centre University College Dublin

Professor Dean A Shepherd - University of Indiana

Dr Jason Cope (late) - Lancaster University

Professor Dr Enno Masurel - Amsterdam Centre for Entrepreneurship

Dr Kenneth A. Grant and Dr Sean Wise

David Harvey Senior Lecturer - University of Huddersfield

Mikkel Draebye Professor of Entrepreneurship -SDA Bocconi School Università Carlo Cattaneo

Paul and Paula Misipeka LABS Restart Smart Australia

T. Harv Ekker - Speed Wealth

The E-Myth Revisited Michael E Gerber

Rich Dad Poor Dad Robert Kiyosaki

The Goal – Eliyah Goldratt

www.ingramcontent.com/pod-product-compliance
Lightning Source LLC
Chambersburg PA
CBHW020923180526
45163CB00007B/2855

www.ingramcontent.com/pod-product-compliance
Lightning Source LLC
Chambersburg PA
CBHW020923180526
45163CB00007B/2855